How To Become A
WORLD-CLASS TRAINING FACILITATOR & COACH

Practical tips and ideas on how to lead a learning and development process

Copyright © 2021

How to Become a World-Class Training Facilitator & Coach
Practical tips and ideas on how to lead a learning and development process
Candido Segarra

ISBN: 978-1-944265-70-0

FIRST EDITION

The views and opinions expressed in this book are the sole expression and opinion of the author, which is based on the personal and practical experience of the author on the matters contained within this book and does not necessarily reflect the opinion, position or views of Foresight Publishing Co., which does not endorse or warranty any claims expressed by the author or contained within this book.

All rights reserved. This book is protected by the copyright laws of the United States of America. This book may not be copied or reprinted for commercial gain or profit. Permission will be granted upon request. No part of this book may be reproduced without written permission, except for brief quotations in books and critical reviews.

For information, contact
Foresight Publishers, Co
Chattanooga, TN 37419

FORESIGHT BOOK PUBLISHING
ForesightPublishingNow.com
Info@ForesightPublishingNow.com

DEDICATION

*To my life and business partner, my wife Cathy,
for her many years of unconditional love and dedication*

*To our loyal customers who have helped make
Foresight the great company it is today.*

TABLE OF CONTENTS

INTRODUCTION 1

SEVEN MODERN MANAGERIAL LEADERSHIP MISTAKEN ASSUMPTIONS 5

    What is a Facilitator? 13
        Competencies, Skills & Characteristics of Effective Facilitators 13
        Right Practices a Facilitator is Expected to Have 15
        Facilitator Versus Instructor 16

    How Adults Learn Best from Any Learning Experience 19

    How to Facilitate Discussions 23

    The Importance of Neutrality in Facilitation 31
        Keeping Track on 5 Main Types of Unconscious Bias in Facilitation 33

    Five Types of Unconscious Bias 35
        How to Avoid Bias at Each Step of Facilitation 36

    Facilitating Content Flow 44
        Useful Facilitation Tips 43

    How Facilitators Can Inspire Participant Engagement 49
        Participant Responsibilities for Successful Meetings 51
        How to Facilitate to Different Types of Personalities 53
        The Types of Facilitators We Despise (Avoid Turning into One) 58

FACILITATING CASE STUDIES 61
Tips on Preparing and Facilitating Case Studies 62
Seven Additional Tips on How to Analyze a Case Study 65

A Typical Session Agenda for An Effective Program 69
Delivery Tips 71
How to Ask Probing Questions 73
Types of Questions to Ask 74
Sample Questions You Can Use During Facilitation or Coaching 75

THE PURPOSE AND ROLE OF COACHING 79
Synergistic Benefits of Coaching 81
Types of Coaching 82
Coaching vs. Micromanaging 83

Steps to Effective Behavior Coaching 87
Additional Coaching Tips 91
How to Provide Corrective Behavioral Feedback 93

PERSONAL PRESENCE: MORE TIPS ON PRESENTING YOURSELF TO YOUR AUDIENCE FOR MAXIMUM IMPACT 97
How to Look Like a True Professional 98
What is Business Casual? 100

The Practice of Good Communication and Presentation Skills 105
How Active Listening Can Strengthen Organizations 107
Ineffective Listening Examples 107
Critical and Crucial Dialogues 108

Basic Guidelines for Designing a Presentation 111
Organization of the Presentation 111

Why Use the Flip Chart 115
Facilitation Using Virtual Meeting Rooms™ 116
Guidelines for Mastering the Use of Video Conferencing for Distance Learning 117

Written Communication 123
Tips to Help You Navigate the World of Business Written Communications 123
Use of Letters vs. E-mail vs. Texting 125

References 129

INTRODUCTION

The worldwide pandemic of 2020-21 forced businesses to close and creatively re-think how to conduct business to survive and thrive. One of the areas significantly affected has been the inability to train and develop the human asset at all levels. Training rooms and venues have been inaccessible as well as professional conferences worldwide were canceled to avoid the spread of the COVID-19 virus. Remote work and online learning became the norm and standard training practices were halted. Due to the pandemic impacting budgets, training initiatives were more intensely scrutinized, where businesses looked for measurable behavior changes and a tangible return on the investment.

While unintended, but positively impacted, changes have been adopted and trending in various organizations, including the surge in management practices such as the "Manager as a Coach" practice. Leaders from around the world are training and learning how to develop internal coaches from their leadership ranks, in order to lead the learning and development efforts for their organizations. In January 2021, the *Wall Street Journal* reported:

THE WALL STREET JOURNAL.

TRENDING IN MANAGEMENT
The Role of the Manager as a Coach and Nurturer

April 16, 2021

"A different model of the boss is emerging as changes are taking place in the economy—a coach and nurturer, not necessarily a business whiz. Managers going forward are going to be less technical experts and more social-emotional experts, to help employees navigate the culture of the organization," says *Brian Kropp of Gartner Research*. As the past decade's trend is accelerated by organizational changes driven by the coronavirus pandemic, including remote work, he expects that managers will continue overseeing increasing numbers of employees in coming years. However, *the role of the modern manager is shifting from authority figure to coach and nurturer*, which means that how managers learn and grow will need to change, too. While management training has traditionally focused on educating leaders to run the business, in modern times it needs to be geared toward training executives to manage through, and in some cases drive, rapid change. The tools it takes to achieve and successfully lead and navigate change are often the tools of a coach and less the tools of a commander.

"Under this new and emerging modern management paradigm, the senior leadership will play an active role as coaches and people developers, with the primary responsibility of inspiring change and improving processes."

It is my hope that this book will teach leaders how to become world-class training facilitators/coaches by developing participative management skills, in order to elevate the competencies of managerial and supervisory teams at all levels.

Embracing the "Manager as a Coach" concept will help leaders transition from managing employees as authority figures in a traditional environment, into the new era of modern managerial leader.

I've tried to combine my thirty years at the forefront of developing senior-level leaders, researching, designing, deploying, and successfully conducting management and leadership training programs and it is my wish that you will benefit from the ideas contained in this book and embrace the "Manager as a Coach" and mentor practice.

– Candido Segarra

SEVEN MODERN MANAGERIAL LEADERSHIP MISTAKEN ASSUMPTIONS

No More Business as Usual

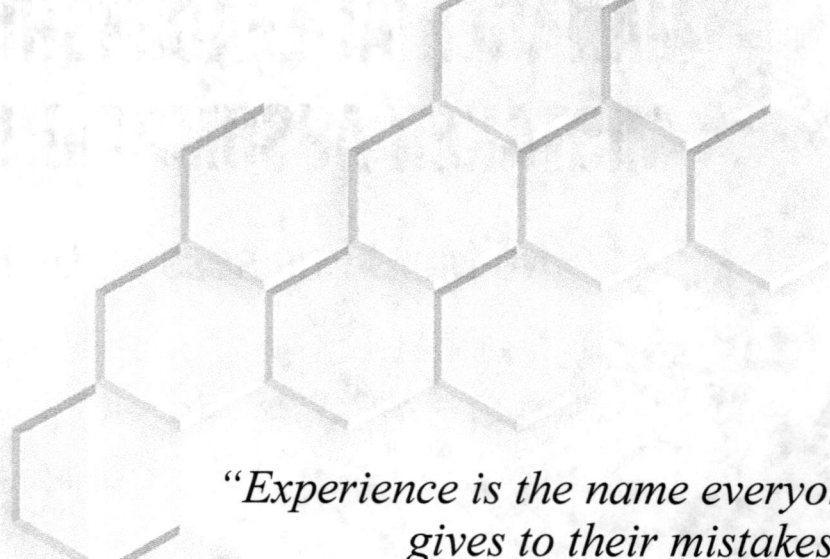

"Experience is the name everyone gives to their mistakes."

– Oscar Wilde

1. Training is a lower-level priority.

2. The loyalty delusion that your current leaders will stay with your company indefinitely.

3. Believing senior leaders do not benefit from conventional training initiatives.

4. You are expecting to manage your organization in the same way as before the pandemic.

5. Managing remotely does not require a new set of leadership skills.

6. Refusing to embrace the modern managerial transition from boss to leader.

7. Ignoring the three main elements that will increase growth within your organization.

When we think about developing managerial leaders, we sometimes, have some rooted assumptions on how that should look like. At a senior management level, many times we think that training and coaching is someone else's responsibility and task within the organization. The following are seven modern managerial leadership mistaken assumptions, which can obstruct an organization's growth and forward thinking:

1. **Training is a lower-level priority.** Embracing the myth that training is an optional "good to have" activity conducted by other people in the organization, or that it is "necessary, but not a priority right now for us", is a paradigm which is not embraced by today's, younger talent. More supplementary training, coaching, and mentoring is expected by younger contemporary leaders than from any previous generation before them in the workplace. If an organizations does not value (or offer) learning, coaching, mentoring, and advancement opportunities, nor embrace these things as part of the corporate culture as essential employee benefits, then your competitors certainly will.

2. **The loyalty delusion that your current leaders will stay with your company indefinitely.** Training and development programs are crucial to individual and organizational success and talent retention. Current company leaders want a safe, healthy, and productive work environment. However, they also need to believe in their company's mission and know they will learn, grow, and thrive with the company. If they feel like their success is in jeopardy, they will look outside the company for further opportunities.

3. **Believing senior leaders do not benefit from conventional training initiatives.** I have often heard senior leadership embrace the myth: *"Management training is good for the staff, but senior managers*

have the skills and experience to lead people, thus, training is not a priority." Training and development are not just about teaching experienced managers new management skills, but it is about sharpening their own current abilities by participating and leading team training initiatives across all management levels. *Senior managers leading a team training process offers exponential benefits, as they get to know intimately the issues affecting the productivity, moral, and needs of their people, which in turn, helps senior managers become more effective and trusted leaders.*

This is the basis of the **Manager as a Coach and Mentor,** which is rapidly becoming the new norm in modern management. The Manager as a Coach and Mentor is a powerful tool through individual and group learning, teaching, coaching, supporting, and leading workgroups to their next-level of personal and team growth.

4. **Expecting to manage your organization in the same way as before the pandemic.** Applying pre-pandemic managerial leadership training practices may be misguided thinking. A recent Garter poll concluded that 48% of employees will work remotely at least part-time after COVID-19 versus the 30% before the pandemic (Baker 2020). New technologies and practices are being embraced by organizations to make remote workplace operations possible. As a result, training has taken a shift toward more participative discussions and less lecturing as well as managers serving as coaches and mentors in the talent development process. The old paradigm of managing based on a hierarchical model or "top down" has become "old school", particularly in keeping cohesiveness among younger generations of talent who are working hybrid, both on-site and remote environments.

How to Become a World-Class Training Facilitator & Coach

5. **Managing remotely does not require a new set of leadership skills.** As organizations were forced to shift towards remote work, managers discovered the critical proficiencies employees and leaders need to collaborate digitally to maintain cohesiveness of teams among workgroups. Modern leaders must learn how to modify performance, goal setting, employee evaluations, project management, team building, training and growth employee satisfaction, adjusting to the new and emerging post COVID-19 workplace and beyond.

6. **Refusing to embrace the modern managerial transition from boss to leader.** We are at a cultural crossroads, where managers need to transition from rulers to leaders, the main difference being how well they collaborate and help develop their teams. Leaders do not need to be technical experts or authority figures to take on the active role of coaches, nurturers, and people developers, nor for changing how managers learn, grow, and teach.

7. **Ignoring the three main elements that will increase growth within your organization: People, Process, and Things.** *People*, being your employees, *processes*, meaning the inner workings and protocols of your organization, and *things*, which are the resources to make it all happen such as equipment, software, technology, etc. These tools make the company more efficient and productive. When leadership inspires their employees to be motivated from within, they will assist you with the other two essential growth elements.

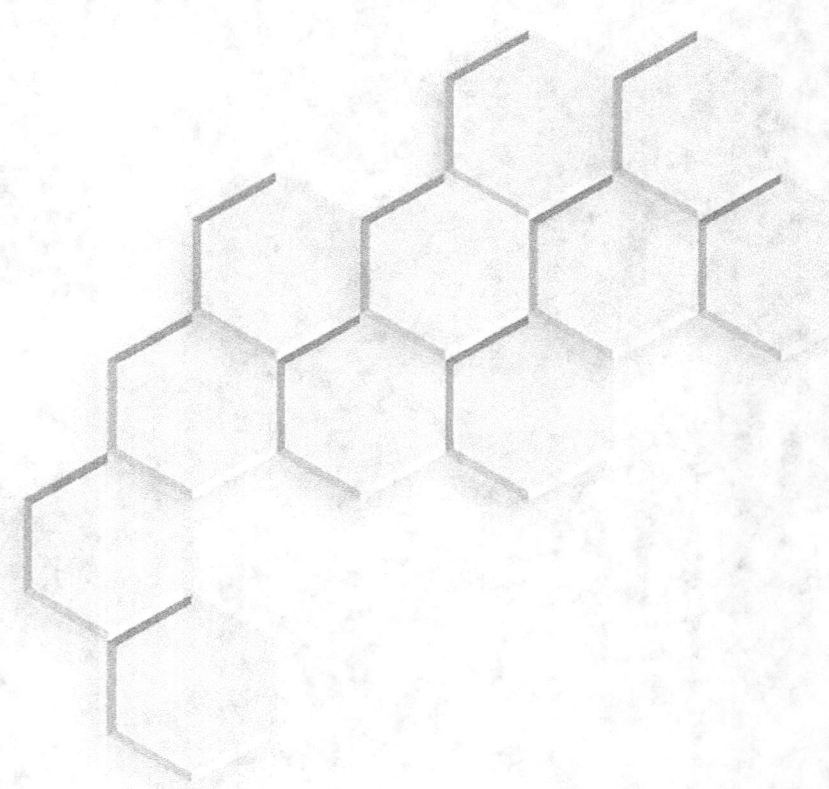

What is a Facilitator?

A facilitator helps bring about a desired outcome, such as furthered learning or increased productivity or communication, by providing indirect guidance throughout a learning process. A facilitator's job is to help manage a process of information exchange. While an expert's role is to offer the content of the discussion, the facilitator's role is assisting with the flow of information and assure participation and group engagement.

Competencies, Skills & Characteristics of Effective Facilitators

If you are involved in facilitation, even if you have never called it that, you might want to consider the competencies and characteristics of an effective facilitator, as outlined by the *Institute of Canadian Cultural Affairs International* (2019):

- Distinguishes process from content
- Is articulate and dynamic
- Manages client relationships and comes thoroughly prepared
- Uses their time and space intentionally
- Is skilled in evoking participation and creativity
- Accomplished in honoring the group and affirming its wisdom
- Capable of maintaining objectivity
- Skilled in reading the underlying dynamics of the group
- Works through challenges in the process
- Adapts to changing situations
- Assumes (or shares) responsibility for the group journey
- Demonstrates professionalism, self-confidence, and authenticity
- Maintains personal integrity
- Studies the topic they are facilitating
- Asks rather than tells
- Offers personal compliments
- Willing to spend time in building relationships rather than always being task oriented
- Initiates conversation rather than waiting for someone else to
- Asks for other's opinions rather than always having to offer their own
- Negotiates rather than dictate decision-making

- Listens without interrupting
- Is emotive, but able to be restrained when the situation requires it
- Draws energy from outside themselves rather than from within
- Has sufficient self-confidence to make eye contact while speaking
- More persuasive than sequential
- More enthusiastic than systematic
- More outgoing than serious
- A counselor rather than a sergeant
- A coach rather than a scientist
- Naturally curious about people, things, and life in general
- Can keep the big picture in mind while working on the nitty-gritty

Right Practices a Facilitator is Expected to Have

1. Must prepare for training delivery at least two weeks prior.
2. Consistently creates a positive learning environment.
3. Establishes credibility as a facilitator without sounding boastful.
4. Adapts teaching to accommodate those who will be learning.
5. Stays focused on learning objectives.
6. Promotes learning by encouraging participation.
7. Always employs a variety of teaching tools and techniques.
8. Can ensure positive learning outcomes.

Facilitator Versus Instructor

An instructor is a content delivery resource; they control what is taught and when. Most information content experts share their knowledge through writing or lectures. When they instruct, they often appear as the "wise guy on the stage," imparting knowledge to passive participants. It becomes the participant's responsibility to learn new skills by adapting and using any prior knowledge they may have to understand the information that the content deliverer is providing.

Facilitators are expert process managers first and then, a content resource. They use their extensive knowledge of participants' different learning styles to create a constructive environment that embraces a participant's prior knowledge and utilizes the unique way individuals learn. A Facilitator's role is to motivate participants to take charge of their learning and encourage a knowledge transfer.

Facilitators complete rigorous qualifications and are continuously engaged in activities that enhance their effectiveness at aiding knowledge transfer, including a rich repertoire of openers, closers, energizers, and interactive lecture techniques. Even though they are Facilitators by title, they are also instructors and can apply either teaching style based on participants' needs and the subject of the course.

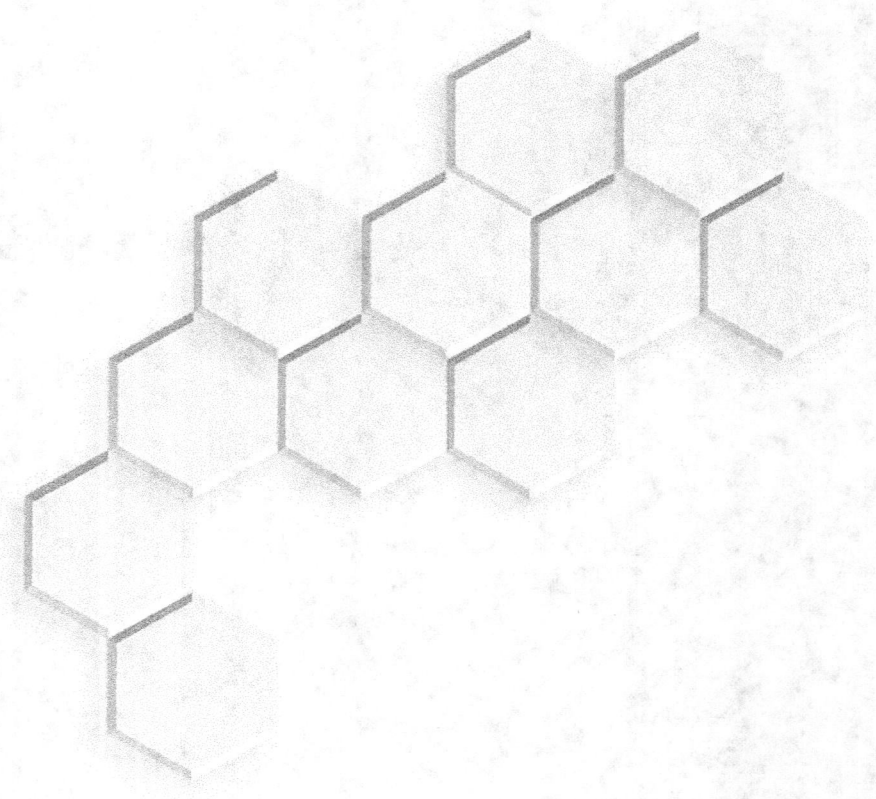

How Adults Learn Best from Any Learning Experience

Adults learn best in certain conditions; it is well established that this is contrary to traditional, instructor-led classes. Malcolm Knowles popularized "andragogy" as the Theory of Adult Learning, the method of teaching adult learners (Kurt 20201). Conditions that are stated as principles of andragogy, which are woven into successful adult learning environments are:

1. Adults want to learn to cope with real-life situations.

2. Adults learn best when they take charge of their learning.

3. Adults engage in learning with unique and often extensive prior knowledge that will either aid or inhibits learning.

4. Adults who test and apply new knowledge and skills within their learning environment are more likely to change their behavior or habitual practices on the job.

5. Adults prefer learning activities that tell what, why, and how.

6. Adults like to know how to apply learned concepts to their work situations.

7. Adults need to be actively involved in the learning.

8. Adult learners are self-directed; therefore, portions of education should be as well.

9. Adult learning is generally more problem-centered rather than subject-centered.

10. The information must be practicably connected to life experiences.

11. The information must be relevant to everyday work needs.

12. Must be well-organized.

13. Adult participants must have time to voice opinions and personal experiences.

14. Adults learn best when challenged.

15. Adults need time to practice new skills.

16. Adult groups like to find common ground and shared meaning.

17. Part of the learning should be experiential (practical, realistic, applicable to their workplace).

18. Learning should be ongoing where concepts can be reinforced and expanded.

19. Adults are more internally motivated rather than externally motivated.

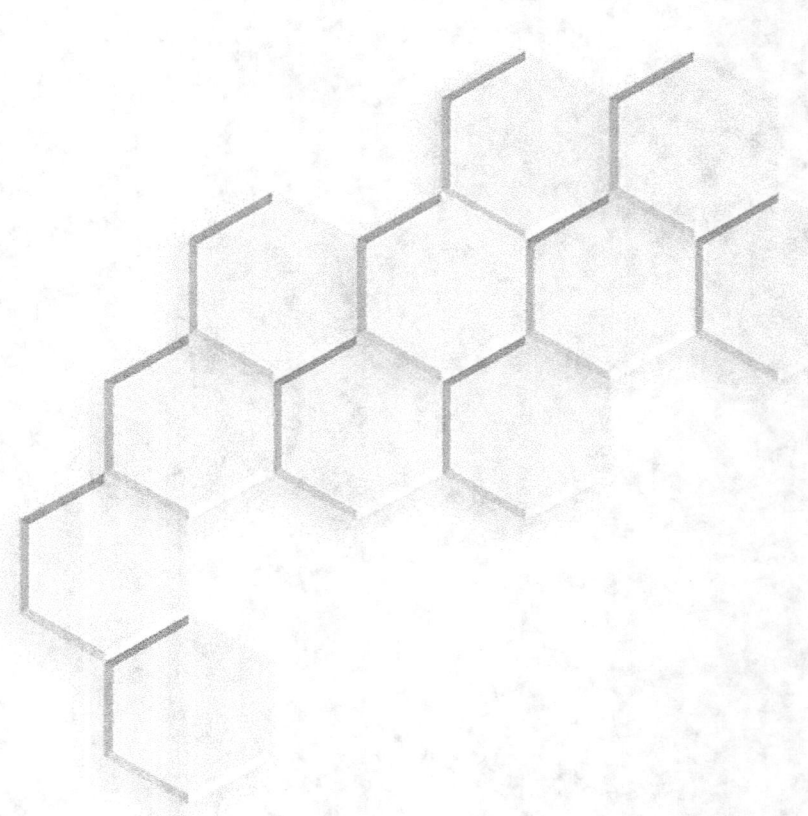

How to Facilitate Discussions

The role of a Facilitator is to draw from the knowledge of the participants and build upon it in order to keep the discussion relevant, on task, and on time. Shorthand for "facilitator of learning," a Facilitator's role is to draw from the experience, ideas, and knowledge of all the participants involved.

An exceptional Facilitator does not just instruct, based on his own experience, but promotes learning from and by the participants. According to UC San Diego (2020), here are some ways for a Facilitator to provide guidance and structure for productive meetings in the class or workplace:

> **1** Understanding the Role of the Facilitator

> **2** Provide Structure to the Discussion

> **3** Guide the Discussion

> **4** Record the Discussion in a Visible Way

> **5** Ensure Productive Group Behaviors

> **6** Summarize the Results

1. **Understanding the Role of the Facilitator**

    - Stay neutral. Your role is to create the process and conditions that enable a group to discuss, plan, decide, learn, and grow. Conduct the discussion without trying to direct the group to a particular outcome, however, you can share your own experiences as related to the subject matter.

    - Achieve learning objectives. Unlike instructors, facilitators are entirely neutral but should still strive to bring out the voices in the group. They must save "teaching" behaviors until the group has explored the subject thoroughly.

    Note: If you must participate, change hats by letting the group know you are shifting roles and will participate briefly.

2. Provide Structure to the Discussion

- Warm up with a topic-relevant ice breaker. After the icebreaker, an open discussion helps participants get involved immediately to address the discussion at hand.

- Structure the discussion, rather than allowing a free-for-all, to ensure greater participation.

Examples:

a. **Round Robin:** Each person speaks in turn.

b. **Nominal Group Techniques:** Each person takes 30 to 90 seconds to collect their thoughts, followed by a round-robin.

c. **Small-Group Discussions:** Break big groups (more than 8) into smaller groups and then discuss the subject. Smaller groups ensure greater individual participation.

3. Guide the Discussion

- Focus on the group process. Is the group repeating itself? Are all the members who wish to participate present? Is the discussion staying on track and on time?

- Explain what you see happening and ask participants to confirm if their experiences are the same. Be factual and specific. Avoid blaming or criticizing individuals.

- Summarize what is being said. In a low-level summary, you repeat what was said back to the group, whereas, in a high-level summary, you tell the group what you believe their discussion means. After a high-level summary, always confirm your interpretation with the speaker(s).

Low-Level Summary Example: "Mike agrees with Linda, this suggestion would be far too costly."

High-Level Summary Example: "So Mike, you seem to be concerned about what this determination means for the future of this project, correct?"

Note: After a high-level summary, confirm your interpretation is correct with the speaker(s).

4. Record the Discussion in a Visible Way

- Use flipcharts, PowerPoint, or meeting software to project onto a screen by the Facilitator or assistant.

- Flipcharts and PowerPoint slides can help record minutes of the discussed points, supplement minutes, or follow up tasks.

- Having the discussion visible helps the group see the progress being made and is helpful when referring to earlier comments.

Note: If possible, use the speaker's words and record everyone's comments to avoid tension or resistance.

5. Ensure Productive Group Behaviors

- Agree on expectations for the group, such as: beginning on time, arriving prepared, and working toward a consensus. Refer to the agreements, when necessary, to keep the group on task.

- Include everyone and ensure all members have an opportunity to speak and be heard.

- Look for common grounds.

- Deal with conflict by discussing the facts.

Example:

"It seems like we have a difference of opinion."

"Let's hear both points of view and continue until we have reached a consensus everyone can agree with."

"What do we know about the situation and what concern do others have?"

"How does the current situation affect your ability to make this decision?"

- Ask for feedback to ensure you are helping the group achieve its goals.

6. Summarize the Results

- Summarize the key points at the of the session for:

    Learning: What information did you gather explicitly related to the learning objectives?

    Follow-up: What can you do to further your learning in the topic(s) discussed?

    Future action: How are you going to implement the skills you learned?

Retention Rates for Different Training Methods

According to Kelly (2012), research from the learning pyramid shows the following average retention rates for different training methods:

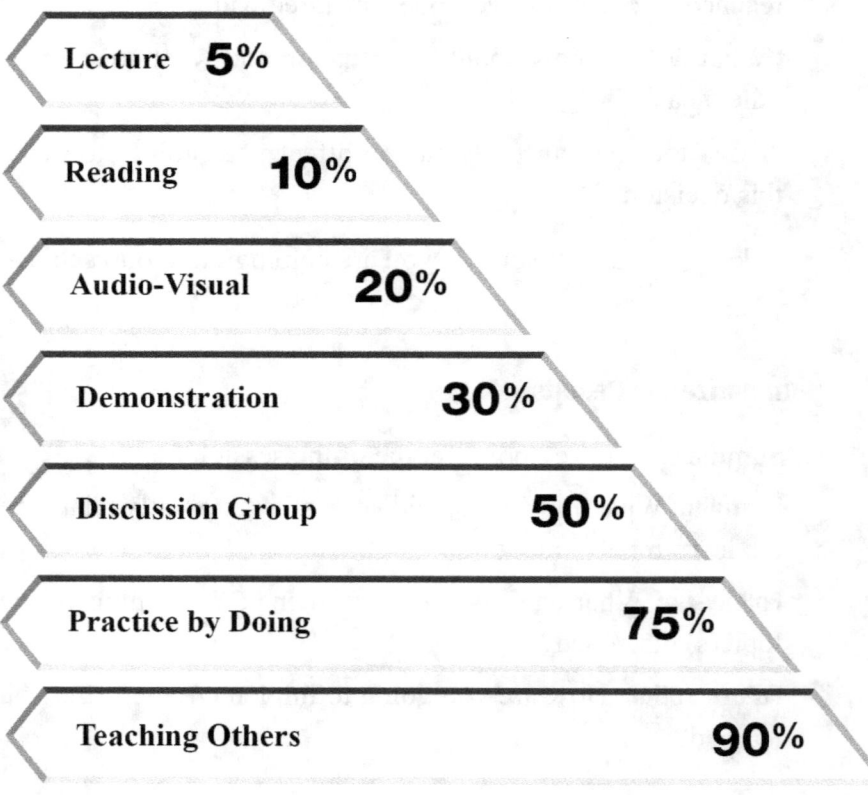

- **Discussion Group:** Discussion is a model of *Cooperative Learning*. It can also be a form of active study, leading to excellent retention of information and attaining higher academic achievement. Unlike competitive or individualistic approaches to learning and studying, a discussion is an arrangement that relies on learners interacting and studying material with other learners and instructors. Discussion Groups stimulate student thinking and increase participation and engagement. Discussions can happen within a classroom setting or by forming small groups.

- **Practice by Doing:** Practice by doing is a model of ***Discover Learning.*** This process of study assists students with taking what they have learned and putting it to use. Performing the action, fosters a deeper understanding and moves this information from short-term to long-term memory. Practice by doing also makes elements of the task more personal, thereby, more meaningful. Practice by doing leads to a more in-depth understanding of the material, more excellent retention, and better recall.

- **Teaching Others:** According to the Learning Pyramid, learners can retain about 90% of what they learn by teaching it to others. If you can teach others accurately, you should have mastered the concepts and have superior retention and recall. The most suitable place to teach others is within a study group. Peer-to-peer teaching should always be part of a productive study group, and each group member should take the opportunity to teach.

The Importance of Neutrality in Facilitation

Facilitators promote evidence-based practices (EBP) approaches that take subjective points of view and are backed by objective basis or facts of support. When challenges of general agreement arise, the most important attribute of a professional Facilitator is neutrality. Facilitators who remain impartial and who speak authentically bring balance and integrity to the meeting space and participants will respond likewise.

- **Practice neutrality when dealing with diverse possibilities.** Do not engage with either side specifically. Do not align with any political or ideological stance.

- **Avoid Leading.** Do not insert your personal opinions into the discussion. Stay away from pointed questions, examples, and analogies can lead the group to think in a certain way.

- **Encourage and affirm each person.** In training we are used to responding to contributions with, "Excellent Point," "Superb," or "Interesting," especially when we hear ideologies that align with our own. This unintentionally makes someone who participates, but does not get the same verbal affirmation, feel like their point was valued less. A content-neutral Facilitator should respond similarly to every point made with "Fine" or "Okay, anyone else?" Display an attitude of acceptance of various point of view. Also, attempt to draw out the quiet participants and the unheard perspectives.

- **Explain your role.** The job of the Facilitator is to share your passion about certain methods, output, or outcomes. Present knowledge in the form of workshops or discussion groups and apply content expertise in the form of questions to foster learning among peers. The Facilitator is charged with maintaining the balance of the discussion.

- **Be aware of your own "unconscious" behavior and biases.** Unconscious biases are learned stereotypes that are automatic, unintentional, deeply ingrained, universal, and able to influence behavior.

- **Resist the temptation to step out of the role of Facilitator.** Being neutral means letting go of the ego and the personal stakes in the outcome of the situation. Make sure to speak in terms of "we" instead of "I." By using "my idea" or "my plan" will discourage contributions.

Keeping Track on 5 Main Types of Unconscious Bias in Facilitation

According to Wolowiec (2019), unconscious biases may be more prevalent when multitasking or working under pressure. When we facilitate, so much information circling in our heads, it is not uncommon for these biases to sneak into our meetings or training sessions.

Unfortunately, this can be detrimental to participation and the outcome of the facilitated experience. If we genuinely value inclusion, we need to be aware of our unconscious biases and do what needs to be done to counteract its negative consequences.

Let's take a deeper dive into unconscious bias that can exists.

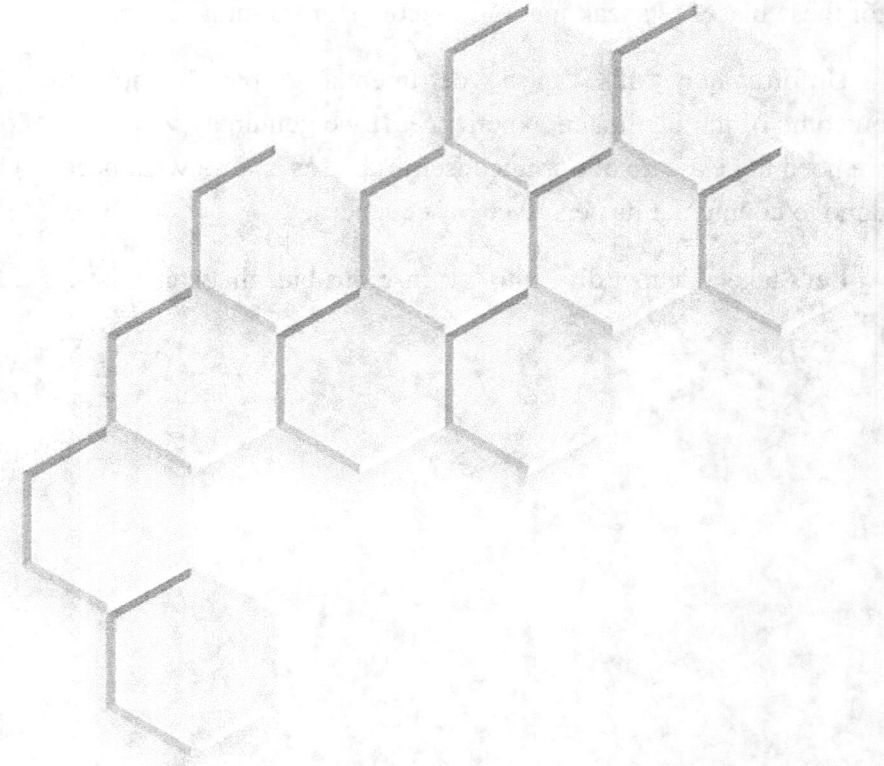

Five Types of Unconscious Bias

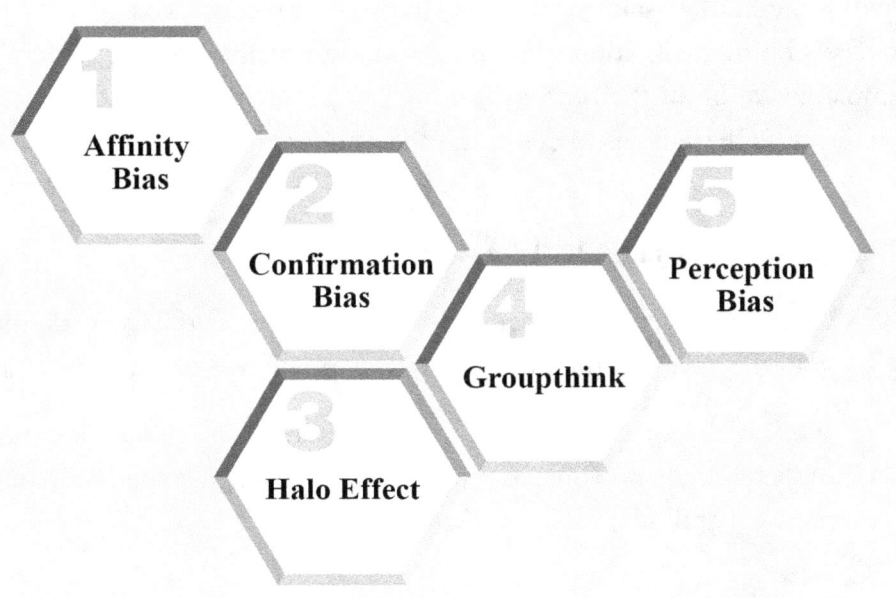

1. **Affinity Bias:** The tendency to gravitate toward and reaffirm those who share similar beliefs and/or backgrounds.

2. **Confirmation Bias:** The tendency to search for or favor information that reinforces pre-existing biases and assumptions.

3. **Halo Effect:** The tendency to use a positive trait as a determining factor for other non-related areas.

4. **Groupthink:** Withholding thoughts or opinions in hopes of maintaining harmony, which results in poor decision-making.

5. **Perception Bias:** Stereotyping or the tendency to assign someone preconceived attributes based on demographic groups they belong to.

How to Avoid Bias at Each Step of Facilitation

Now that you are aware of the 5 main types of unconscious biases, Wolowiec (2019) said you can easily avoid preconceived notions in every step of facilitation, through the design of the process (before), implementation of the process (during), and evaluation of the process (after). Use these types to create a respectful learning environment:

Design (before facilitation)

- Consider each type of unconscious bias and intentionally work into your design opportunities to be aware of and overcome them.

- Work with key leaders to get a clear picture of the social identities of the participants (For example: race, gender, age, experience, and physical abilities).

- Use this information to raise your consciousness about the effects of power and position rank privilege, how it will affect participation, and to further explain and direct your concepts and discussions.

- On the day of the facilitation, before the session is set to begin, placing yourself in the shoes of the participants and check-in with yourself anticipating the following answers to these questions:

    - What is one thing I have experienced today that could affect my performance?

    - What am I feeling at this moment?

    - What impact could my experiences and emotions have on today's session?

    - What objectives can improve the quality of participation in today's meeting?

Implementation (during facilitation)

- While it is imperative to monitor *all* participant's involvement throughout the session, it is especially important for traditionally marginalized groups (for example: people of color, younger participants with less experience, women, LQBTQ+, and people with disabilities) to be *equally* heard and be included within the discussion.

- Behaviors to monitor, be aware of and correct:

    - Who are you repeatedly calling upon?

    - What voices are dominating the conversation?

    - Who appears to be the least comfortable speaking up?

How to Become a World-Class Training Facilitator & Coach

- What perspectives are not being shared?
- Who is taking upon the leadership roles when separated into small groups?

• Addressing any bias behavior immediately coming from yourself or other participants will create a safe and productive learning environment.

Evaluation (after the facilitation)

• Following the facilitation, it is important to self-reflect in the outcomes using the following questions as a guide to evaluate the session and your role within it:

- What is one thing related to diversity, equality, and inclusion I was mindful of as I was facilitating?
- What is one thing I observed in the meeting related to diversity, equality, and inclusion?
- What is one success I observed related to diversity, equality, and inclusion?
- What is one challenge or opportunity presented that is related to diversity, equality, and inclusion?
- What were the effects of privilege on participation?
- What did I do specifically to create a more inclusive environment?
- What is one thing related to diversity, equality, and inclusion I will do differently the next time I facilitate?

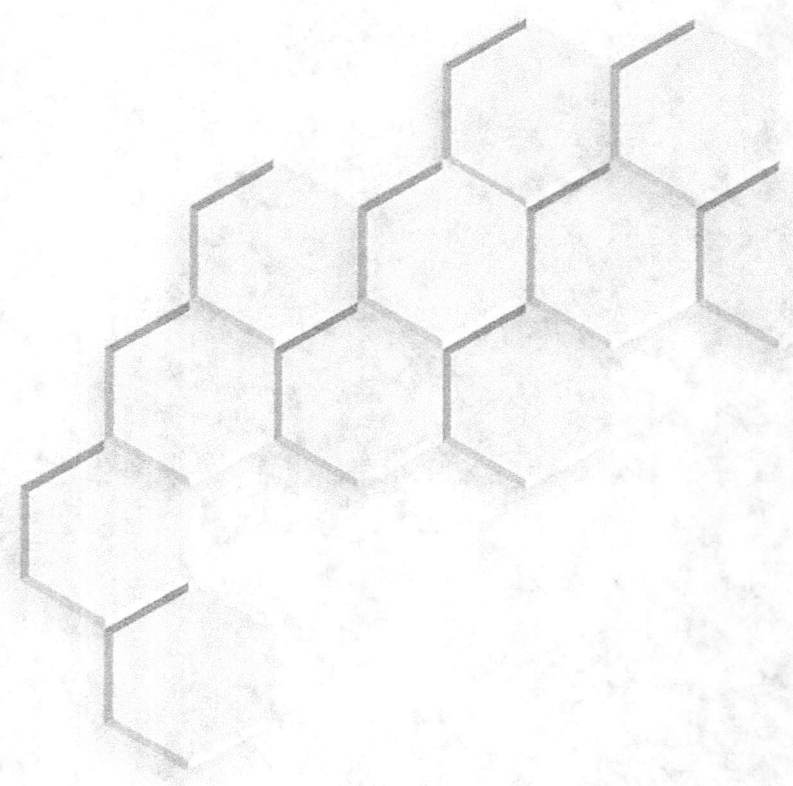

Facilitating Content Flow

The introduction of information is always a part of the facilitation process. Although there are many ways to introduce content, a typical flow is as follows:

- **Challenge:** This can be a question, thought-provoking story, an example, a set of facts or statistics, a shared experience or metaphor, but must give enough context to allow sufficient time to have a healthy, meaningful discussion.

- **Discussion:** Use a variety of conversational strategies and provide plenty of opportunities for learners to participate. Encourage everyone to participate and ask for their wisdom and experiences during the discussions.

- **Focus:** Keep discussion on task. Narrow the scope of the conversation and encourage the group to get to the topic's core. Provide clarity of goals and remind the participants of the rewards of success. Remind the group that they have a limited amount of set time for their answers, so discussions do not drag.

- **Exemplify:** This step highlights the transition from Boss to Facilitator because the intake of collective wisdom is much more likely to solve a problem than the Boss's experience alone. As a Facilitator, you can demonstrate with examples, provide *complementary facts*, or participate in an activity, but overall, you are enabling the group to learn from the experience and wisdom of one another.

- **Synthesize:** Annotate (flip chart) and highlight the most relevant and widely accepted responses. Facilitators can be viewed as a catalyst for discussion and makes possible the transformation of input (participants' ideas and opinions) into the desired outcome (refined ideas, decisions, strategies) without being an active part of the discussion.

- **Understanding:** Deliver and discuss content, and then summarize key points to ensure everyone comprehends what was discussed. It is essential to have the participants articulate understanding by paraphrasing what they have learned.

- **Practice:** Use small group discussions to examine learning objectives or real-life application exercises where participants can observe what they have learned.

- **Transition:** Shift gears and move onto the next activity or content segment of the agenda. The participants must understand where they have been, where they are going, and why it makes sense to go in that direction.

- **Close:** End a meeting with energy and commitment. When you are closing a meeting, it means you have accomplished your learning objectives, and it is time for developing realistic action plans to implement right after the session. Get in the habit of reviewing accomplishments at the end of each meeting. The more you affirm success, the more momentum you will create.

Useful Facilitation Tips

- **Always be on time.** Start your sessions promptly at promised time, whether with one or fifty participants are present. Establish a precedent for punctuality even before you start your sessions. Lock the door once you begin the session. This sends a message to latecomers that disrespecting the Facilitator and the participants who chose to be professional and on time, will not be tolerated.

- **Always be prepared.** Nothing will speak to your professionalism more than being prepared, in command of the material, and ready to deliver. The preparation for the day should include: (1) having all training materials on each participant's seat, (2) setting up the PowerPoint presentation on the screen, (3) doing a sound check (if applicable), and (4) reviewing the material before presenting.

- **Clarify meeting expectations.** As part of your introduction opening, outline their responsibilities as a participant, your role as a Facilitator, and communicate exactly what is needed to have a successful meeting.

- **Establish clear objectives.** Have appropriate meeting objectives that translate into goals for your meeting. Create a productive plan or agenda and present these points at the beginning of the session as "learning goals," and then work towards accomplishing them.

- **Allow participants to learn from one another.** The primary goal of facilitation or Participative Learning is for professional adults to learn from each other's experiences and expertise. Our job as Facilitators is to make sure we further the discussion and manage the learning process to achieve the goal of exchanging information within the group.

- **Promote participant involvement.** Engagement is the key to adult learning and to the application of concepts discussed, in the workplace. Use all the tools presented in this book to invite and ensure all the participants contribute to the process.

- **Enforce positive and respectful interaction.** Lead by example. Be respectful and reinforce courteous interactions. Look for opportunities to connect and engage others in a way that will build self-esteem.

- **Summarize and clarify complex content or discussions.** Rephrase complex ideas to ensure complete understanding. Outline the discussion in a flip chart and go over the summary at the conclusion of the meeting to increase retention (see page 54 on listening skills).

- **Ask open-ended questions and actively listen.** Using open-ended questions naturally drives the conversation and active listening when a response is given demonstrates a desire to reach a solution using a collaborative approach (see page 79 on open-ended questions).

- **Respect participants time.** Be aware of pacing, speak enthusiastically to keep engagement. Keep the conversation moving and on-task. Keep an eye on the clock and end your sessions on time.

- **Clarify with examples, but do not overshare.** Keep personal and professional stories, even related to the topic, short and appropriate. Check your ego at the door and stay humble when sharing.

- **Encourage participants to share their ideas.** Ask for ideas on ways they can relate to issues discussed and implement solutions in their workplace.

- **Maintain a balance of content and process.** Relaying content is important, but never interrupt the process if a discussion in high gear. However, make sure conversations are not repeating.

- **Include various activities.** Small group or team activities work best when discussing a case or trying to come up with workplace solutions. Activities that outline a step-by-step process to implement the topic concepts are always most welcomed by participants.

- **Offer encouragement, praise, and recognition.** But do not offer random praise. Recognition specifically related to something they have done well, will provide encouragement to continue down the same path. Asking a person to share their expertise with the group is another way to offer praise because it shows you respect their knowledge and experience.

- **Design your material geared to your audience and then challenge them.** With your group's objective firmly in mind, preparation for the meeting is of the upmost importance. Your job as a Facilitator is to choose and design the right group process experience and develop an effective agenda for participants to reach their desired outcome.

- **Organize your content.** Be sure your presentation has a beginning, middle and end. When arranging a discussion, center all talking points and activities around your main learning objectives. Create a syllabus, which can be an effective tool for helping participants approach their learning because it can provide a quick overview of the topics of discussion and goals of the discussion.

- **Understand people learn in different ways.** According to Calvert (2011) introducing information in a variety of ways can keep participants engaged by appealing to the six preferred learning styles of adults:

    1. **Visual:** These learners need simple, easy to process diagrams, or written words. Infographics in PowerPoint presentations and flipcharts are beneficial to this type of learner.

    2. **Auditory:** These learners need to hear the information to process it. They may prefer to read written material aloud and enjoy lectured learning.

    3. **Print:** These learners need to write down information to process it. They take excellent notes but may never review them later.

    4. **Interactive:** These learners need to talk about the learned concepts. Small groups discussions and Q&A formats help this type of learning. Case study method and group discussions will suit well for these types of learners.

    5. **Tactile:** These learners need a hand-on experience to learn. They tend to avoid written instructions and dive right into to attempting to working it out with their hands. Simulations and role plays will go well with these types of learners.

    6. **Kinesthetic:** These learners learn through movement. Training exercises and role playing supports this mode of learning. Also, giving them the freedom to stand and move around also aid in their learning.

- **Encourage constructive differences of opinion.** Always remain neutral and accepting to everyone's ideas. Remember to consider diverse points of view as equally valid and worth pondering.

- **Keep participation balanced.** Do not allow individuals to dominate the conversation. Make sure everyone is participating within the discussion, taking turns sharing ideas, and not straying too far from the topic.

- **Pay attention to participant reactions, moods, and attentiveness.** As a Facilitator, you are like a cop directing traffic. You need to read the flow, timing, and value of the discussion. Make sure everyone contributes to the discussion in a way that drives it forward and in a respectful manner.

- **Get agreement on group actions.** Before leaving the room, make sure everyone agrees on what actions they are planning to take to implement and transfer the learned concepts into the workplace.

- **At closure, confirm your call to action.** Make sure participants create and write down an action plan on how and when they are going to implement the main concepts or ideas (what) discussed in the session.

- **Solicit authentic evaluations.** Encourage them to write sincere evaluations. Communicate the importance of honest feedback to evaluate the learning concepts and improve the delivery of the session.

How Facilitators Can Inspire Participant Engagement

Participation equals engagement, and when learners participate in the discussion, their relationship to the subject matter intensifies and becomes more authentic.

Each person in the meeting room has a unique perspective that can cause others to reevaluate their own. When specific viewpoints remain unexpressed, the group losses that value it could have added to the conversation.

People want to add value and speaking within groups is a powerful way to be heard. Here are some ways that you, as a Facilitator, can inspire participant engagement:

- **Make learning relevant.** Adult learners need to see how the knowledge will improve their life outside the learning environment. If they do not understand how this information will enhance their work performance or help them master a new skill, they will not be invested in the material you are trying to relay. While organizing your discussion and choosing the perfect graphics to incorporate into your presentation, keep in mind how they reinforce the primary learning objectives.

- **Include activities that encourage the learner to explore.** Adults understand and retain more information when they are active participants in their own learning process. Create activities that encourage them to explore the subject matter in their own way and learn from personal experiences.

- **Always consider the experience and educational backgrounds.** Adult learners have life experience and have established a broader knowledge base than younger learners. When designing your presentation, you should take their experiences and education into account to fully engage your audience. When organizing your content, ask yourself:

    – What is the highest level of education they have completed?

    – What tasks are they accustomed to performing on the job?

    – Are they well-versed in the technical jargon of their profession?

- **Offer immediate feedback to allow participants to learn from mistakes.** When participants make an error or need an alternative approach to problem-solving, offering immediate, constructive feedback is essential. This will provide an opportunity to learn from mistakes and see the direct consequences of changing course.

- **Incorporate emotionally driven content.** When participants feel emotionally connected to the subject, they will likely be more engaged resulting in more retain information. Use images that are powerful and relevant to the topic of discussion that evokes a certain feeling. Positive emotional elements can inspire and motivate learners who may otherwise feel disconnected from the learning environment.

- **Cognitive Overload is real.** Break your content into a smaller block of information to avoid straining mental capacity. Our short-term memory can only retain a small amount of information simultaneously. So, the more information that is delivered at once, the less likely participants are to recall it later. Try bullet points, numbered lists, or smaller bursts of information on a specific topic.

- **Practice makes perfect.** Use practice exercises to ensure participants fully comprehend the material. Repetition is crucial, so develop tasks that remind them of key points throughout the session.

Participant Responsibilities for Successful Meetings

Share the following suggestions with your participants the day before the session to inform them of the reasonable expectations set to have an effective meeting:

1. Be courteous to the Facilitator and other participants, regardless of their views.

2. Be truthful but respectful when delivering information or formulating an opinion.

3. Offer context, corroborating information, and facts to support your opinions.

4. Be open- minded and willing to accept other people's views.

5. Listen carefully (for intent and content) to what others are saying.

6. Conduct discussions with a positive attitude and a spirit of learning.

7. Attack issues and problems, not people.

8. Ask questions and encourage others when they speak.

9. Do not dominate the discussion.

10. Do not forget about (natural) humor, however, do not fake humor.

11. Ask follow-up questions specifically related to the discussion.

12. Volunteer your participation and do your part for the good of the group.

13. Paraphrase what you think the Facilitator is saying to demonstrate understanding.

14. Be committed to having an excellent meeting

15. Understand that effective meetings are empowering.

How to Facilitate to Different Types of Personalities

As we coach individuals, we need to consider the wide variety of personalities and characters we will encounter. Some participants may be tiresome, while others will be exciting. In either case, you can use their behaviors to your benefit as a Facilitator as well as your participants.

It is common to have one verbally dominant participant within the group. Use this individual to your advantage by asking questions when participation is winding down. This is the perfect opportunity to inform the group you will be jumping in and asking questions to help further the discussion.

Also, remind participants several times throughout the session to speak right to the heart of the issue to save time and energize the discussions. If someone continues to dominate the discussion, this may be the right time to break into smaller groups, whether in person or virtual.

Throughout your journey of group and teamwork, you may meet some of these problematic participants:

1. The "Know-it-All" or "Challenger"

Usually, there is one person in the room that thinks they have more experience than the Facilitator. This may very well be the case; however, it should not diminish your ability to keep control of the process. They may question everything you say, but as a coach, you must reinforce that you are not the expert; they actually are. Recognize their experience by asking exploratory questions such as: "Can you explain that idea in more detail?" "In your opinion, what makes that idea unique?"

In Chinese martial arts, there is the principle that calls for leaving the opponent's attack line, so their blow only finds the void and, if possible, hit them in the same direction of their movement. You can use this same principle in facilitation. Let the "know-it-all" be part of the process for a brief time, unopposed, before turning the room to another participant, after making a statement like: "Dan, thank you for sharing this principle, it certainly adds a lot to what we said; let us hear from another team member and amplify what Dan said."

Using this technique will give Dan his desired recognition before shifting the attention to another participant and away from him. Return to Dan periodically during the discussion to hear his opinion. This should keep him away from sabotaging your presentation with "wise" interruptions.

Remember, we are in the front of the room to facilitate the discussion and help adults learn from each other, not spread our wisdom through lectures or as experts in the subject matter. Focus only on your audience's ideas, knowledge, and experience, while staying away from your own; this is the true experience of *participative learning*.

The "I Don't Want to be Here," or the "Shy" Participant

You can recognize this type of participant because they are typically distracted or withdrawn. Some of the leading causes of this behavior are:

- **Boredom.**
  They do not feel challenged by either the process or the Facilitator.

- **Shyness and insecurity.**
  They are hoping for that you do not call them.

- **Anxiety.**
  Their anxious mind is distracted with problems at work or home.

The best way to challenge the Shy Participant is to make them active members in the process by:

a. periodically asking them questions about their experiences in the subject matter.

b. praising their responses.

c. asking them to help the group by being scribes and making annotations on the whiteboard.

The shy or quiet participant may work better in a small group discussion, paired exercises, or individual reflection activities. Include a variety of ways for participants to engage, reflect, and learn. Never confuse quietness with lack of engagement.

3. The "Microphone Hugger"

They confuse a 30-second answer for an hour dissertation. This is another version of the "Know-it-All," and you can diffuse them by cautiously interrupting their extended response by acknowledging the value of their statement, taking the microphone (or focus) away from them, and asking another participant for their opinion.

4. The "Super-Achiever"

These individuals can pose a challenge for Facilitators because their endless achievements may cause feelings of inadequacy in other group members. Within your group, it is important to reinforce "wins" and successes happen at different stages for everyone. Having the Super-Achiever share their experiences on how they achieved success can become a source of inspiration for the other team members, giving them new ideas and insights.

5. The "Joker"

Humor can provide lightness within the coaching process. Joking can help spotlight key points while keeping the conversation casual. The joker makes their impact on the group with their comedy, but may take it to an extreme, so be aware of the consequences on the session. Also, using humor, the Facilitator can let them how they are impacting the group with the frequency of their jokes ("Peter you seem to have missed your call as a stand-up comedian").

6. The "Devil's Advocate"

The Devil's Advocate can guide the group into a rich territory of different perspectives. Their opinions and participation remind us there are many different points of view, which exist within different topics and groups of people. Questions like: *What is the flip side of this? What important alternate viewpoint do they raise that we have not discussed?*

7. The "Argumentative One"

Some difficult participants may want to argue just for argument's sake. A great question to ask could be: *What is the main objective of your argument?* Another approach is to defer the issue being argued to the group. If several people in the group agree, then it may be worth discussing further. If not, the group can move on.

8. The "Sidebar"

Although it frequently occurs in smaller groups, the "sidebar" conversation happens when two group members engage in their own exchange while others are trying to speak. If an open invitation to share with the group does redirect the sidebar conversation back to the broader group space, physically move and stand near where the conversation is happening. Be genuinely curious and invite the sidebar pair to share with the rest of the group.

The Types of Facilitators We Despise
(Avoid Turning into One)

We have all been to workshops or meetings run by poor Facilitators, which can drive us nuts. When you encounter one of these unfavorable Facilitator types listed below, you know there is a long day ahead. As you continue your journey as a coach or Facilitator, be aware of yourself and your teaching styles, so you do not become what you despise.

- **The Drill Sergeant:**
  The Facilitator who is rigid, follows agenda exactly as written, and always puts the clock above content.

- **The Guardian:**
  The Facilitator who makes certain all conversations go through them and not from participant to participant.

- **The Know-it-All:**
  The Facilitator who always has the answer and cannot bring themselves to say, "I don't know."

- **The Ice Cube:**
  The distant and aloof Facilitator who is unwilling to add an emotionality or personalize the experience.

- **The Blabber:**
  The Facilitator who loves the sound of their own voice and goes off on tangents, where no one else can get a word in.

- **The Pretender:**
  The Facilitator who does not ask any real questions, only "pretense questions," designed to give them an excuse to brag.

- **The "I Can't Hear You" Type:**
  The Facilitator who refuses to listen when others are speaking.

- **The "Marathoner":**
  The Facilitator who wants to get everything done, now. They plan several activities, do not allow breaks, and ignores the importance of reflection time for the group, before moving on to the next item on the agenda.

- **The Parrot:**
  The Facilitator who repeatedly restates information and summarizes the obvious.

- **The "Molasses" Type:**
  The Facilitator who is painfully slow and does not recognize the appropriate pacing for need for variety and style to keep the group engaged.

- **The Passenger:**
  The Facilitator who lets participants dominate the discussion and gives up the reins of facilitation.

- **The Storyteller:**
  The Facilitator who tells far too many personal stories and never really gets to the content.

- **The Centerpiece:**
  The Facilitator who makes themself the topic of discussion in the workshop.

- **The Tunnel Driver:**
  The Facilitator who repeats his actions hour after hour.

The case method was introduced by Christopher Columbus Langdell, Dean of Harvard Law School from 1870 to 1895. Langdell conceived of a way to systematize and simplify legal education by focusing on previous case law that furthered principles or doctrines.

FACILITATING CASE STUDIES

Harvard Business School adopted the case study method, which discusses real-life situations business executives have faced. As participants, the mission is to study the facts of the case and share alternative ways to solve the issues outlined using prior knowledge and experiences to validate how the protagonist(s) approached the problem, or how the participants would approach and solve the problems outlined in the case.

This method promotes participant engagement and the use of peer discussions to solve problems in real life. Analytical skills such as critical thinking and decision-making are crucial when handling certain situations in real-time such as in a boardroom with peers, discussing concerns, and suggesting solutions.

Tips on Preparing and Facilitating Case Studies

1. **Get familiarized with the facts of the case.**

    Read the first few paragraphs and then browse the rest of the case. Each case begins with a fact description, many times supported by exhibits. <u>Ask yourself:</u> *What is this case about, and what information should I review further?*

2. **Re-read the case, underline important text, and make margin notes.**

    Walk around in the shoes of the case character and own that individual's problem. Focus on the key aspects of the case. <u>Ask yourself:</u> *What critical points are being raised? What fundamental problem is this executive trying to resolve?*

3. **Take notes about key points and review again the facts.**

   Highlight relevant considerations and perform a quantitative or qualitative analysis of the facts. <u>Ask yourself:</u> *What recommendations should I make based on my case data analysis? How would I react if I encountered the same situation?*

4. **Re-read the case study several times.**

   Upon first inspection, you should read for the basic details. In the preliminary stages of analyzing a case study, no detail is insignificant. With each reading that follows, you should look for more information about one specific topic such as: competitors, business strategy, management structure, financial loss. Dig deep and find unnoticed variables that drive a situation. Use a highlighter to make important passages stand out and take notes. Look for phrases and relevant information about the facts of the case.

5. **Understand the details of the case.**

   The Facilitator will observe how well the participants comprehend both the business aspects and main facts of the case before leading a discussion on addressing alternate solutions and making tough decisions. Remember, the content of the case study is what is most important, not how the information is presented or the peculiarities of its style.

6. **Gather in small groups.**

   Before you open the discussion to the entire assembly, split up into various discussion groups. When participants work in small teams and converse with their very accomplished peers from diverse functions and industries, many unique perspectives are brought to the table. Others begin to see there are many ways to solve the same problem.

7. **Start an open discussion.**

    Within the open classroom discussion, the Facilitator should *guide* the conversation by asking questions about relevant facts, issues, and alternate solutions, without providing answers. The participants must interact in the classroom with their peers—analyzing the data, debating the issue(s), suggesting new viewpoints, proposing alternate positions, and building upon one another's ideas. Remember, participants should not re-write the case by providing data and facts that were not specifically provided.

8. **Be yourself.**

    Above all, be yourself. Do not try to imitate your former professor or favorite motivational speaker's style when facilitating a case discussion. Do not feel like the participants expect you to be a guru on a particular topic, in the contents of the case. You are the guide, and *they* are the experts analyzing and proposing solutions.

Seven Additional Tips on How to Analyze a Case Study

Case studies are descriptions of management situations. They usually include information about the setting like the location, type of organization, size, and sector. They also present essential background information on the case. These steps will guide you through the process of analyzing a business case study:

1. **Analyze and explain the business environment related to the case study.**

    Describe in detail the nature of the organization and its competitors. Provide general information about the specific market and clientele. Take note of any significant changes in the environment or any new business endeavors.

2. **Describe the structure and size of the central business under consideration.**

    Provide figures on employment. Examine their managerial composition and provide an overview of leaders and chain of command, include details of ownership and investment holdings. Detail annual earning, profit, and financial history.

3. **Pinpoint the key issue or problem in the case study.**

    Several different factors may be involved but examine critical elements and regard what is mentioned most throughout the data provided. The focus should be on the business's central issues: a change in clientele, market expansion, or creating a marketing campaign in response to a competitor.

4. **Describe how the business acts in response to these issues or problems.**

   Use the information you collected and create a timeline of steps you plan to take. Remember to include critical data from the case study: purchasing a new property, revenue stream changes, and increased market spending. Explain whether each step of your response was an effective solution for the identified problem.

5. **Point to successes, failures, unpredictable results, and inadequate measures.**

   Suggest alternative or improved measures the business could take and use specific examples with data collection and calculations made to support your suggestions.

6. **Describe what changes need to be made in the business to arrive at the measures proposed.**

   Include detailed modifications that need to occur involving the organization, strategy, and management to reach the intended solution.

7. **Conclude analysis by reviewing findings and emphasizing what should be done differently within the case.**

   Discuss the formulated business plans that showcase the participants understanding of the case study. Review solutions, how they will be implemented, and if any changes could be made to the plan to increase efficiency.

A Typical Session Agenda for An Effective Training Program

- **Welcome Opening Statement:** Welcome the participants and introduce the topic describing the importance of the subject and its relevance to their workplace.

- **Learning Objectives:** With the PowerPoint, state the learning objectives for the session.

- **Icebreaker:** Conduct an icebreaker to loosen up the audience and prepare them for the topic. Always make a direct connection between the icebreaker and the topic of discussion. In my experience, group discussions and exercises related to the subject matter far better than silly games.

- **Session Opener/Open Discussion:** Ask relevant questions to spark discussion about the topic. This will help participants learn from each other as they discuss the subject based on their experiences, points of view, and diverse professional backgrounds.

- **Instruction:** Develop an example or a short comment expanding on the content of each PowerPoint slide, or an analogy to add to the instruction section, so it does not look like you are just reading off information. The comments can be based on:
  - Examples from personal experience
  - Historic, business, or world event accounts
  - Recent news headlines
  - Experiential workplace accounts

- **Exercises:** Make sure everyone participates equally. Always keep control of the meeting, limit each participant's time, and make certain comments are constructive. Involve the shy participants by inviting them to share their opinion.

- **Outline Learned Concepts:** Summarize critical points they learned on a slide at the conclusion of the PowerPoint presentation. Adults learn by repetition; that is why we must summarize at the beginning and again at the end.

- **Discussion of Personal Action Point(s):** Explain the assigned Personal Action Point(s) for the topic, which needs to be implemented within the next four to six weeks, and progress will be discussed within the subsequent one to two Video Coaching (or internal coaching) sessions.

- **Closing Statement:** Make an encouraging closing statement or use an impactful, inspirational closing story, which reinforces the topic you had discussed.

- **Session Evaluations:** Ask participants to fill out and return their Session Evaluations.

The following guidelines will help you prepare and to facilitate a management development training program session:

- Read and carefully study the Participant's Workbook twice. There is no substitute for preparation which is the key to success and a quality presentation. Never become arrogant, as to think you do not need to review the material beforehand or prepare written notes to guide you through the discussion. Overconfidence is the fastest and surest way to failure.

- Start preparing at least one week before each session. You should be completely ready to conduct the facilitation two days before the event. This will give you time to do a final review and build confidence.

- Develop and practice powerful opening and closing statements, related to the topic at hand.

- Study the discussion questions and select those most relevant to the debriefing, or those that can spark a specific group discussion.

Delivery Tips

- The way you present yourself begins before you have a chance to say your first word. Be aware of your body language, your wardrobe, and how your audience perceives you. Practice good posture and stand with your feet shoulder-width apart. Avoid being stiff and avoid fidgeting.

- If you speak to a small group of about 2-15 people, try to establish eye contact with each person for a few seconds throughout your delivery.

- Prepare a presenter's outline from your PowerPoint presentation in font size 20 and glance at it every 5-10 seconds. Remember to look at your audience most of the time, not at your notes.

- Speak slightly louder and slower than you usually would when talking to a friend. An excellent way to practice these guidelines is to speak along with a news anchor when watching television.

- Adjust the volume, rate of your speech, and gestures to the size of your audience and age group. A lot of energy and animation will work better with a younger audience. While a more serious, yet enthusiastic tone is more effective when speaking in front of more mature audiences. Always remember, a monotone voice is poisonous to the attention of an audience.

- The expansion of the vocabulary we chose is crucial to professional success. Avoid offensive slang or foul language. Street language does not portray toughness or show that you are trendy. Instead, it exposes weakness and a limited vocabulary and, people will treat you accordingly. Therefore, the first step to good communication is to improve your vocabulary. Include industry-based jargon and commit to looking in the dictionary and learn a new word every day.

How to Ask Probing Questions

Facilitators ask questions for a variety of purposes, including:

- To actively involve participants in the lesson
- To increase motivation or interest
- To evaluate participants' preparation
- To check on the completion of an application
- To strengthen critical-thinking
- To re-examine previous lessons
- To encourage further insights
- To evaluate mastery of goals and objectives
- To promote independent learning

A Facilitator may have different purposes for asking questions during a single lesson, or a single question may a variety of reasons it is being asked. In general, research shows that instruction involving questioning is more effective than instruction without questioning (Marzano et al. 2000).

Questions that focus learners' attention on essential elements of a lesson result in better comprehension than those focusing on unusual or interesting aspects. Questions should also be structured to elicit correct responses.

Types of Questions to Ask

Instructors usually classify questions according to Bloom's Taxonomy (Bloom et al. 1975), a hierarchy of increasingly complex intellectual skills which includes six categories:

- **Knowledge:**
  involves recalling data, information, methods, or processes

- **Comprehension:**
  understanding meaning about what is being communicated and using the ideas without relating it to other materials or seeing its fullest effects

- **Application:**
  the use of abstractions in concrete situations

- **Analysis:**
  the ability to separate concepts into parts and distinguish between facts and inferences

- **Synthesis:**
  involves bringing together elements to form something new

- **Evaluation:**
  capacity to make judgments about the value of ideas and methods for a specific purpose

Some researchers have simplified the classification of questions into lower and higher cognitive questions. *Lower cognitive questions* (fact, closed, direct, and knowledge questions) involve recalling information. *Higher cognitive questions* (open-ended, interpretive, evaluative, inquiry, inferential, and synthesis questions) involve the mental manipulation of data to produce or support an answer.

Extensive use, 50 percent or more, of higher cognitive questions with adult students, is positively related to an increase of:

- ✓ On-task behavior
- ✓ Length of participant responses
- ✓ Number of relevant contributions
- ✓ Number of participant-to-participant interactions
- ✓ Participant use of complete sentences
- ✓ Speculative thinking
- ✓ Relevant questions posed by participant

Sample Questions You Can Use During Facilitation or Coaching

- Do you think that recommendation will work?
- What did you like about that recommendation?
- How are you advancing toward your financial goals for this quarter?
- What is the difference between…?
- How could you use…?
- How would you explain…?
- How do you know…?
- How consistent is…?
- What might have been the result if…?
- What would you do about…?

- What insights can you derive from…?
- What is the main point here?
- What is the critical point of your conflict?
- What would you say to support (or challenge) that point?
- Please provide an example or explain a personal experience to support your viewpoint.
- Could you please explain the supporting factors behind your opinion?
- What experiences might have led a person to perceive an issue in this way?
- What do you think people who hold this belief care deeply about?
- What would be a compelling case against what you just said?
- What do you find most credible about this point of view?
- What about this position can you not endorse?
- What have we overlooked that should be discussed?
- What will you accomplish? What is the timeline?
- What support do you need to guarantee success?
- How will you know you have been successful?
- What knowledge have you gained from this experience?
- How important is this?
- Where do you feel lost?
- What is the intent behind what you are saying?

- What can we do for you?
- What do you think the problem is?
- What is your role in this issue?
- What have you tried so far? What worked? What did not?
- Have you experienced anything like this before? (If so, what did you do?)
- What can you do for yourself?
- What do you hope for?
- What is stopping you from…?
- What would you be willing to give up for that?
- If you could change one thing, what would it be?
- Imagine a future when your problem has been resolved. How did you achieve this?
- What would you like us to ask?
- What have you learned?

How to Paraphrase a Question to Clarify an Answer:

- You are saying…
- In other words, …
- I gather that…
- If I understood what you are saying…

"Coaching is unlocking people's potential to maximize their own performance. It is helping them learn, rather than teaching them."

– Sir John Whitmore

THE PURPOSE AND ROLE OF COACHING

Just like in sports, it is the coach's primary purpose to help take the team, collectively and individually, from where they are, to where they have the potential to be. It is about building the self-esteem and skills of your team, regardless of the issue or task at hand. If leaders are cognizant of the genuine purposes of coaching and act authentically, they will be amazed by the vast improvements in both relationships and performance that will result. Common coaching purposes include:

- To build awareness in a way that empowers choice and leads to change

- To improve motivation and overcome personal obstacles

- To learn new skills and acquire competencies

Let us analyze this other definition: Coaching in the workplace is the art and *practice* of *inspiring*, *encouraging*, and *facilitating* the *performance*, *learning,* and *development* of an employee.

- **Practice:** the application of an idea or belief. Although there is a science to coaching, it is also an artform because when the skill is learned and exercised correctly, the focus is not on technique but on being fully engaged with the learner. Then, the coaching process becomes a conversational exchange in complete harmony and partnership.

- **Inspiring:** causing great emotional or mental stimulation. Coaching is about helping individuals unleash their true potential through raising awareness. By sharing and inspiring new ideas and experiences, it encourages creativity.

- **Encouraging:** igniting hope or uplifting toward a positive outcome. Coaching is about strengthening and supporting the employee through effective communication, soliciting suggestions, and inspiring a proactive attitude.

- **Facilitating:** to guide or make easier. The purpose of coaching is to the instill the belief within the employees/managers/participants that they can think creatively to develop ideas and implement action plans by and for themselves.

- **Performance:** the execution of an action. Anything a coach says or does should be driven by the intention and the spirit to improve performance and achieve greater efficiency.

- **Learning:** acquiring knowledge and skill from instruction. It can also mean studying and then modifying a behavioral tendency by experience, such as by exposure to conditioning. Refers to a broader area, apart from approaching a task or mastering new technology, and should focus on teaching employees to believe in themselves. If managers can act on this primary focus of learning authentically, they will be amazed at the vast improvements in productivity.

- **Development:** to create or produce by deliberate effort over time. It is about looking beyond immediate objectives and focusing on future performance and growth of the employee, both personally and professionally, within the organization.

Synergistic Benefits of Coaching

Synergy is the energy created by working together to perform various processes. Within the business world, it is advantageous to combine two or more elements so that performance is greater and more efficient than the sum of the individual parts. Effective coaching in the workplace should deliver three essential elements: **achievement**, **fulfillment**, and **joy**, from which both individuals and organizations can benefit. These three important components are strongly interconnected because the absence of one will negatively affect the others. Learning without fulfillment is exhausting and, to some, may seem pointless. Fulfillment without further learning will eventually become dull, and the absence of joy will dampen your spirit, so you will have no drive to learn.

- **Achievement:** the delivery of extraordinary results gained by effort. When organizational and individual goals are achieved, and when projects are executed well, it suggests effectiveness, creativity, and innovation.

- **Fulfillment:** the satisfaction of developing one's abilities which includes learning and growth. Through coaching, individuals begin to identify goals that are personally and professionally rewarding, which in turn, increases self-motivation.

- **Joy:** the emotion evoked by success. Enjoyment follows when people achieve their personal and professional goals and when learning is part of the process.

Setting exciting but attainable goals will help the cycle of learning continue. Effective coaching delivers sustainable success and increases performance long-term because the emphasis is placed on developing the confidence of the employee. American businessman Stephen Covey said, *"Motivation is a fire from within. If someone else tries to light that fire under you, chances are, it will burn very briefly."*

Types of Coaching

Giving constructive feedback to anyone is difficult, but coaching can accelerate the development of managers and improve communication within the organization when done correctly. It is widely recognized that both individuals and groups perform better with coaching and this higher level of performance translates into organizational success. Some of the specific ways coaching are beneficial include:

- **Coaching for skills** helps the employee learn specific abilities and perspectives over several weeks or months. The key is to interact with the information, gather quotes from books, videos, podcasts which will help appeal to all types of different learners. One of the most surprising ways to learn is to teach the new information to someone else. This will benefit the organization and its employees because it will create a pyramid of learning.

- **Coaching for performance** focuses on the employee's effectiveness in their current position. Frequently, it involves training for one or more leadership competencies, such as communicating vision, team building, project management, or delegation. Performance Feedback Reviews are the perfect tools to evaluate performance development.

- **Coaching for development** refers to sessions that enhance the executive's competencies required for a future job, career path, or specific role. It can be associated with outplacements, restructuring, future promotions, or a succession plan in the organization.

- **Coaching for the employee's agenda** generally entails working with an employee on any personal or organizational concerns they may have, such as company downsizing or change in vision. Emotionally charged issues are more likely to arise in this type of coaching.

Coaching vs. Micromanaging

Micromanagement as a leadership style will most likely deliver unfavorable results by stifling employee creativity, causing staff to question their self-worth, and restrict productivity.

Although micromanagement can build discipline, it keeps employees locked within a limited range of action. Employees who adapt to a micromanagement style are either rebellious or unable to make any independent decisions, creating even more work for the managers. When micromanagers relax their tight grip and switch to a coaching approach, their employees often flourish because they can finally demonstrate their full potential.

Making a shift from manager to leader is not letting go of the finer details or compromising productivity; instead, it is about trusting employees to handle them. Managers go from doing the work to leading conversations to guide others to do what needs to get done.

Unlike micromanagement, where employees perform to please the demands of their boss, coaching encourages team members to explore and discover how smart they can work to achieve organizational and departmental goals.

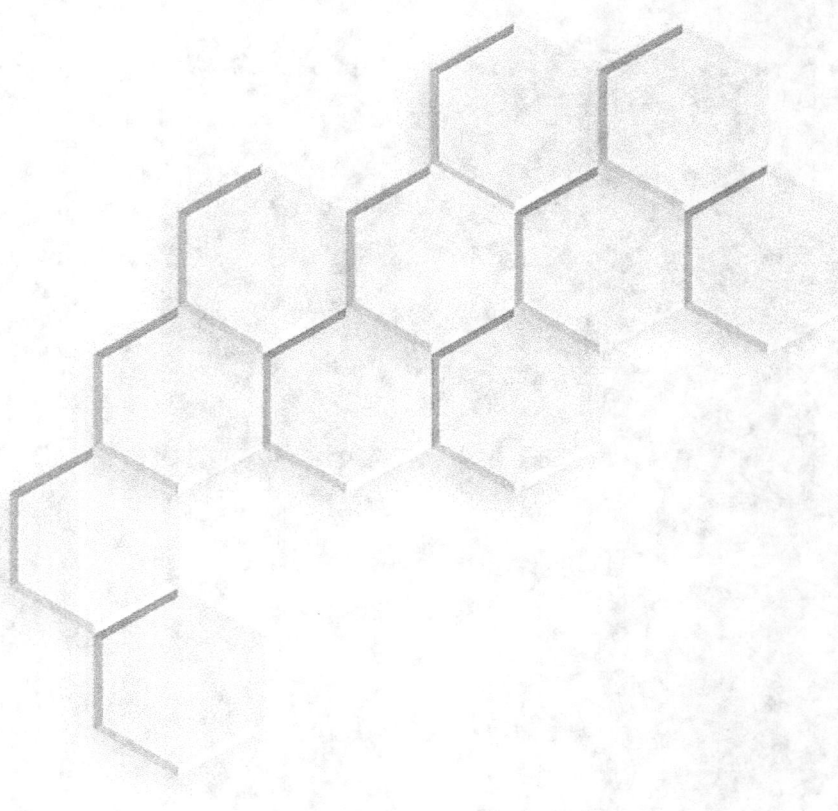

Steps to Effective Behavior Improvement Coaching

1. Build a Relationship of Mutual Trust
2. Open the Meeting
3. Get Agreement
4. Explore Alternatives
5. Get a Commitment to Act
6. Handle Excuses
7. Provide Feedback

Step 1: Relationship of Mutual Trust

The framework of any coaching relationship is in a manager's day-to-day relationship with their employees. Without some degree of trust, leading a productive meeting is unlikely. Mutual trust is one of the most crucial elements that make a successful team. If employees feel trusted by their manager, they also feel valued, making them more inclined to offer extra support and effort to meet company goals.

Step 2: Open the Coaching Meeting

When beginning a meeting, the manager needs to clarify the specific reason for the gathering in a non-accusatory way. The key to this step is to restate in a friendly, non-judgmental manner the meeting purpose. Reasons for the coaching meeting may include:

- Process review and improvement
- Correction of issues for future improvement
- Creative thinking and brainstorming to formulate new ideas
- Goal setting to successfully implement and achieve results in current or future projects
- To serve as a sounding board on diverse issues
- Correction of personal attitudes/disciplines/policy violations, etc. (probably the most difficult)

Step 3: Get Agreement

The most critical step in the meeting process is getting the employee to agree a performance issue exists verbally. A typical managerial mistake is overlooking performance issues with the assumption an employee understands its significance. A manager must define the nature of the issue at hand and lead the employee to recognize the consequences of not changing their behavior (if that is what the coaching meeting is for). To persuade an employee that a performance issue exists, you must identify the behavior or problem at hand which needs to be resolve or improved and explain the consequences if it is not resolved.

The skill of identifying a behavior issue involves three parts. You should:

1. Document explicit instances when performance issues occurred.

2. Clearly explain your performance expectancies within the involved circumstances.

3. Ask the employee for agreement on the subject.

The skill of explaining consequences involves two parts.

You should:

1. Ask the employee to clarify their understanding of the consequences because of the performance issue.

2. Ask the employee to verbalize understanding and compliance in the matter.

Step 4: Explore Alternatives

Investigate ways an issue can be improved or corrected by encouraging the employee to identify different solutions. Avoid interrupting with your alternatives unless the employee is unable to think of any. Push for specific answers to the issue, not generalizations.

Your goal is not to decide on one alternative, but to maximize the number of choices the employee has, you should discuss their advantages and disadvantages.

Promote out-of-the-box thinking when exploring your options because it fosters innovation.

Step 5: Get a Commitment to Act

The next step is to assist the employee with determining an alternative but not choosing them. Whether it be a pledge to make progress or a promise to take the initiative, the manager must get a verbal commitment from the employee regarding what action will be taken and when. Support the employee's choice and offer praise.

Step 6: Handle Excuses

Employee may justify their actions at any point during the coaching meeting. To handle these excuses, take a comment the employee perceives as accusatory and recast it as an encouragement to reevaluate their behavior. Respond empathetically to show support for the employee's situation and communicate an understanding of both the content and emotion behind the employee's comment.

Step 7: Provide Feedback

Effective coaches recognize the importance of giving regular performance feedback to their team, both positive and remedial. There are a few significant points to remember when giving feedback to others. Feedback should:

- Be timely and occur as soon as practical after the interaction or observation is made.

- Be specific in your delivery. Ambiguous or generalized declarations like "You did a wonderful job" or "You didn't care for the clients' concerns well enough" are too vague and do not give enough insight, specifically, into the behavior you would like to see repeated or changed.

- Focus on "what," not "why." Avoid making feedback seem like judgment. Begin with "I have witnessed..." or "I have noticed..." then, refer to the behavior. Focus on action and not the person. Describe what you witnessed and how those behaviors impact the team, client, etc.

- Use a sincere, normal, conversational tone of voice. Avoid a manner that displays anger, irritation, or sarcasm.

Positive feedback improves performance. People will go that extra mile when they feel appreciated. Poorly handled corrective feedback can be a significant source of conflict, but when it is dealt with excellence can improve performance, behavior, and understanding.

Additional Coaching Tips

When a manager can transform their own style from a ruler to a leader, without patronizing, lecturing, or behaving like a parent (talking down), and encouraging conversations between equals (Adult-to-Adult) then the employee grows to their full potential. Here are some effective coaching tips:

- Share stories of your own experiences and how you handled issues.
- State observations of facts, not personal interpretations.
- Set goals to define the behavior you want to see developed.
- Do not tell them what to do. Instead, guide them through the process of making the best decision for themselves by asking questions about alternatives options and outcomes.
- Share insights to spark discussion. ("I have noticed...", "I saw how you dealt with...").

- Share observations about the employee's behavior without sounding condescending.

- Provide suggestions in the form of advice based on how you would handle a specific situation.

- Help them see the value of change by sharing what success will look like and the significance of advancing to the next level.

- Share with them in what capacity you can help them implement their action plan and improve their work habits.

- Focus on solutions by thinking with them by turning conversations into brainstorming and problem-solving session.

- Remain in control of the meeting. Be aware of emotions when discussing controversial issues.

- Focus on defining the course of action or correction with the employee.

- Be helpful by mapping out a course of action to help employees improve their performance.

- Stay firm and let them know the importance of the issue without shying away from your position to obtain agreement.

- Act when you see issues surfacing. The longer you wait, the bigger the problems become, and they harder are to deal with.

- When you are upfront when dealing with issues, the more beneficial your coaching becomes. Remember, confrontation (not conflict) promotes healthy adult-to-adult communication and supports respect.

How to Provide Corrective Behavioral Feedback

Corrective behavioral feedback is information communicated to a learner intended to modify their thinking or behavior for the purpose of improved learning. It is meant to lead a positive change and is an honest attempt to help the recipient improve their performance, behavior, understanding, relationships, or interpersonal skills. Corrective feedback also meets the needs of the organization, to ensure goals, milestones, and timelines are met. It seeks to recognize and modify behaviors falling below organizational standard, so objectives can be met.

For this feedback to have any real changing power, it must be delivered in a way that it will be listened to, instead of just met with defensiveness or anger. The provider of the feedback should be someone the recipient respects and should be delivered as sensitively as possible.

Reasons for Corrective Behavioral Feedback

- To improve an individual's personal development
- To improve relationships between individuals and group
- To improve communication between individuals and group
- To improve performance
- To improve organizational climate
- To improve efficiency of a particular project or activity

How to Deliver Behavioral Corrective Feedback

- **Be respectful.** Delivery should be face-to-face and in a private area to protect privacy of the employee receiving the developmental feedback.

- **Be understanding.** Mistakes happen, and you never know what others are going through in their personal life.

- **Be supportive.** Encourage them. Let them know you believe they can and will be successful.

- **Accountability.** Outline specific expectations and responsibilities for improvement.

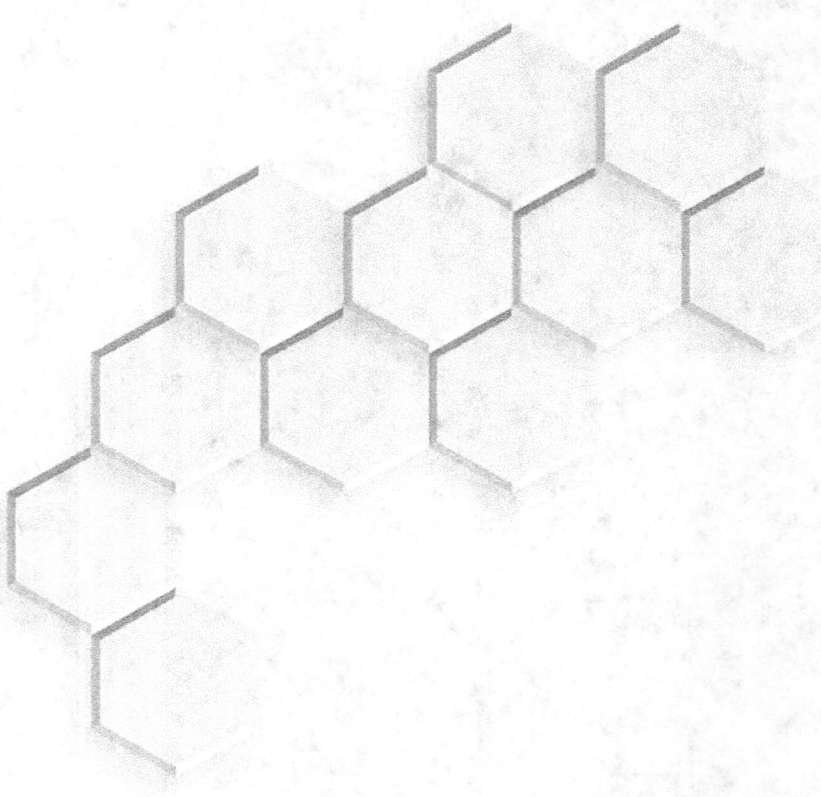

PERSONAL PRESENCE:

More Tips On Presenting Yourself To Your Audience For Maximum Impact

How to Look Like a True Professional

You will never have a second chance at making an excellent first impression. True professionals dress one notch above the company code and their peers. The way you dress affects your attitude. The more informal you dress, the more informal your mindset will be.

Business Attire Do's & Don'ts

Save money in the long run by purchasing quality garments because they wear longer and fit better. If your clothing reflects a professional image, others will respond in that way. Looking the part promises both personal and financial benefits. Here are a few suggestions to dress for success:

Dressing Tips for Men

- Do wear your suit jacket when you are conducting business outside your office. Your authority travels with you.

- Do keep hair and nails clean and neat.

- Do not overpower with heavy cologne.

    Do not wear short-sleeved shirts under suit coats. Showing a clean cuff is a must.

- Do not wear ankle socks or light-colored socks with a dark suit.

Dressing Tips for Women

- Do wear comfortable shoes and hosiery that complement your outfit.

- Do wear natural-looking makeup.

- Do wear appropriate jewelry. Avoid wearing large pieces or costume jewelry.

- Do keep hair and nails neat.
- Do not overpower with heavy perfume.
- Do not wear elaborate hairstyles. Keep it classic and preferable out of the face.
- Do not wear jeans or casual slacks.

Executive Wardrobe Tips for Men

- For Suits, look for:
  - Classic fabrics, patterns, and colors that are always in style and easy to accessorize.
  - Jackets with contoured collars that lie smoothly around the neck with no space between them and your shirt.
  - Smooth, straight seams with a single row of stitching.
- Outer coats: Keep in mind that...
  - Outer coat sleeve length should cover the suit coat sleeve.
  - It would be helpful to sit in your outer coat in the store to be sure it is comfortable.
- Shoes
  - Wear shoes that coordinate with your suit.
  - Keep shoes in good condition and polished.
  - Belt leather should match show color.

Executive Wardrobe Tips for Women

- For Suits/dresses, look for:
  - Classic fabrics, patterns, and colors that are always in style and easy to accessorize.

- Dresses in solid colors or conservative prints.
- Jackets with contoured collars that fit smoothly around the neck with no space between it and your shirt.
- Smooth, straight seams and hems.

- Suit care: Be sure to ...
  - Hang suits on wooden or plastic contour hangers with the jacket unbuttoned and pockets emptied.
  - Leave space between hangers so garments will be free of wrinkles.
  - Read and follow the care instructions on your garment.

- Blouses/shirts: Look for ...
  - Tailored blouses/shirts with minimal frills or ruffles.
  - Solid colors or conservative prints to coordinate with your suit.

- Shoes:
  - Keep shoes clean and in good condition.
  - Classic heels no higher than three inches, loafers, or stylish flats.

What is Business Casual?

Business casual attire can be described as a blend of traditional business wear with a more relaxed style that is still appropriate in a business setting. You are not expected to afford the same clothing as a CEO. However, do invest in quality clothing that will look appropriate for a business casual environment and different professional occasions during your first couple of years on the job.

Everything should be clean, well-pressed, and free from signs of wear and tear. Even the nicest khakis may not be the best choice after they have been put through the wash 100 times.

Use common sense. If you show up and realize you are underdressed, offer a quick apology and then make a good impression with your interpersonal skills.

Specifics for Men's Business Casual

- **Ties:** By dressing nicely, you are paying your host a compliment. Ties are generally unnecessary for business casual occasions, but you can wear a tie if ever in doubt. It never hurts to be slightly overdressed. You can always show up in a tie and scan the room, and if no one else is wearing one, remove yours and place it in your jacket pocket.

- **Pants:** Khaki or dress pants in conservative colors such as navy, black, gray, or camel should be neatly pressed and not crease too much around the ankles. No-break or half-break (A break is the creasing of the fabric where your pant leg meets your shoe) is the best option, but make sure they are well-fitted, so they are not too short when sitting. Dress jeans are also acceptable.

- **Shirts:** Long-sleeved shirts are considered dressier than short-sleeved and are appropriate even in summer. Choosing white or light blue in a solid or conservative stripe is your safest bet. Polo shirts are acceptable in more casual situations but should always be tucked in.

- **Socks:** Wear neutral-colored socks in brown, black, gray, or beige. If patterned, make sure it is subtle and includes both the color of your pants and shoes. Socks should be mid-calf length, so no skin is visible when you sit down.

- **Shoes:** Leather shoes in brown or black should be worn. Sandals, athletic shoes, or hiking boots are generally not appropriate for even casual events in the professional world.

- **Facial Hair:** Just as with interviews, facial hair, if worn, should be well-groomed.

- **Jewelry:** Wear a conservative watch. Removing earrings is always a safe bet.

Specifics for Women's Business Casual

- **Pants/Skirts:** Women can wear fitted casual pants or skirts. For a more business-like appearance, pants should be creased and tailored. If in doubt about the industry standard, observe women on the job, career fairs, information sessions, or other related events.

- **Skirt Lengths:** Skirt length varies from season to season but avoid extreme trends. Hemlines should never be more than a few inches above the knee, and slits should remain modest. The best time to check a hemline is when sitting; also, keep in mind how comfortable you will be doing the mundane such as getting in/out of the car and walking up a flight of stairs.

- **Shirts/Sweaters:** Feel free to play with colors, patterns, and styles with modest necklines. Be sure to pair bold pieces with neutrals. For example, a printed top should be worn with solid black slacks. In addition to tailored shirts, tailored knit sweaters and sweater sets are appropriate business casual choices for women. Sheer fabrics, plunging necklines, and thin-strapped sleeves should be avoided.

- **Jewelry/Accessories:** Wear a conservative watch. Earrings should be simple and above the earlobe. Jewelry and scarf styles come and go, so keep your choices simple and conservative. Avoid extremes in style and color.

- **Cosmetics:** Nails should be trimmed, and if polished, should be a neutral color, especially within conservative industries. Keep makeup simple and appropriate for the daytime.

- **Shoes:** Shoes should be leather or micro-fiber. Regardless of style, stay traditional. Make sure you can walk comfortably in your shoes.

- **Hose:** Hosiery is not essential for business casual but is recommended with shorter skirts and in more formal environments. Trouser socks or knee-high hose are appropriate with slacks.

- **Purse/Bag:** A tailored purse is best and should coordinate with shoe color. A purse that hangs on your shoulder is advantageous, as well, because it frees your hands for greetings, such as handshakes or holding a beverage.

The Practice of Good Communication and Presentation Skills

Of all the attributes a true professional must have in their toolbox, communication tops the list. We spend at least 85% of our waking time communicating in one way or another. So, we need good conversational skills to connect with our spouses, children, bosses, employees, customers, friends, and anyone else we may interact with. A true professional strives to know others well enough to present their ideas effectively.

The Art of Active Listening

Listening is one of the most effective communication tools we possess. It is an important pathway to understanding, and without it, conflict can develop. Active listening is paying attention and giving feedback to another person to ensure mutual comprehension. The goal of active listening is cognitive understanding, which means this type of listening aids with information retention. Here are some tips to make sure you are actively listening:

1. Give your full attention to the speaker. Show you care by putting off all other activities, physical or mental. Absolutely no texting.

2. Make eye contact, nod as you listen, and keep body language open by uncrossing your arms and legs.

3. Do not try to plan out your response. Hear out what they are trying to tell you.

4. Show to the speaker that you know what they are saying by using verbal replies, like "I understand," "Really?" and "I see," as well as responding nonverbally with nods and expressions of interest.

5. Do not constantly repeat the thoughts expressed to prove you were listening.

6. Occasionally rephrase the ideas presented or ask questions that demonstrate you understand what was said. The difference between these two intents communicates different messages to the speaker.

7. Silence is okay. Many people become nervous when the conversation comes to a standstill and struggle to fill the empty spaces. With active listening, you hear and retain more information, so sometimes people need a moment to digest the information before they respond.

8. Show the communicator respect by connecting more effectively by adjusting your tone of voice, rate of speech, and word choice to express sympathy, interest, and compassion for what they have to say.

9. Ask thoughtful, open-ended questions to encourage them to continue sharing.

How Active Listening Can Strengthen Organizations

Active listening can increase participant/employee engagement at each level of the organization. When people feel heard, understood, and respected it increases trust and boosts morale which is critical for course correction in a rapidly changing business environment. Active listening has several benefits to your organization, such as:

- ✓ Promotes better business communications
- ✓ Helps teams improve communication skills.
- ✓ Helps resolve interpersonal conflict.
- ✓ Encourages employees to express their opinions freely.
- ✓ Opens the door to new perspectives, ideas, and possibilities.

Ineffective Listening Examples

Hearing is different from listening; one is processing sound, and the other is processing information. Ineffective listening interrupts the method of gaining and retaining oral information from another person. These practices can have detrimental consequences on task efficiency and workplace relationships:

- **Selective listening** is only listening to the information you, the listener, identify with or are relevant to your own needs.

- **Insulated listening** is the opposite of selective listening and includes ignoring information and avoidance of specific topics.

- **Pseudo listening** is pretending to listen but not enough actually to understand the information presented. Usually, the listener responds with a smile, nod, or minimal verbal acknowledgment but ignoring the listener.

- **Stage Hogging** is listening only to add one's own ideas and opinions to the conversation.

- **Switch Tasking** is listening without full attention while attempting to complete other duties.

Critical and Crucial Dialogues

Many critical and crucial conversations pop up without warning at the least expected moments. These conversations can range from an exchange where bets are high (like in certain negotiations), where opinions are different than ours, or where emotions are strong such as when an irate customer is shouting his complaint.

Some people typically handle these conversations by (1) avoiding them or (2) handling them poorly because they catch them off-guard. You can handle them well if you practice a few rules that will give you the leading edge.

These rules are

1. **Be Compassionate**

    - Restate or paraphrase what you heard the customer say.

    - Ask questions. Make them feel valued.

    - Increase safety by respectfully acknowledging and mirroring the emotions they appear to be feeling.

2. **Be Responsive and Proactive**

    - Agree with the others involved. Once you have reached an agreement, move on. Do not turn an agreement into an argument.

- Build the conversation. Say things such as, "Absolutely. In addition, I noticed that…" and then add elements that were left out of the discussion.

- Compare differing points by saying, "I think I see things differently. Let me describe how."

3. Be Competent

- When someone brings attention to a problem, immediately take ownership, formulate a creative solution, and then discuss how you will resolve it.

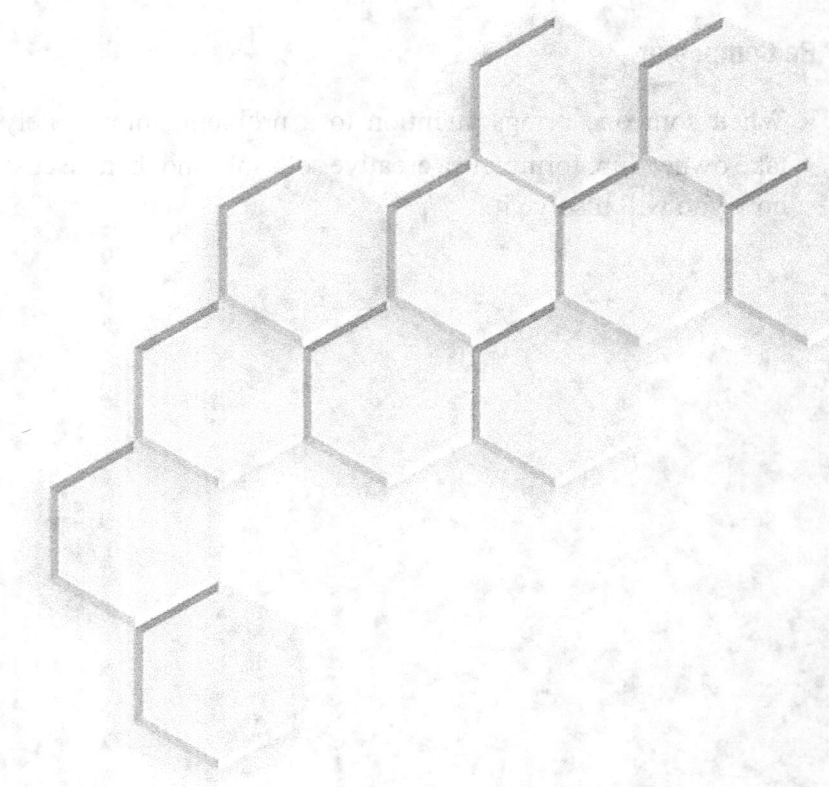

Basic Guidelines for Designing a Presentation

Whether you are making a sales pitch, introducing a new idea, proposing a budget, business, or marketing plan, or giving a major speech to an audience, there much to be quickly gained or lost from a presentation depends on your preparation and delivery. A little bit of skill and a lot of practice will go a long way toward making a highly effective presentation.

Organization of the Presentation

1. List the top three goals you want to accomplish with your audience. Make sure the points you wish to present are concise and meet each of the goals you want to achieve. It could be quite easy for your audience to completely miss the point of your presentation if it lacks focus. For example, your goals may be for them to appreciate the quality and features of your new products

and learn how to use them. Remember, your goals are based on what you want from your audience.

2. Clearly define who your audience is and why they need to be at your presentation. Your audience will want to know right away why their attendance is important and ensure that your presentation makes this clear to them right away. This information will also help you clarify your invitation list and design your invitation specifically with them in mind.

3. List the significant points of information you want to convey to your audience. When you are done making that list, ask yourself, "If everyone in the audience understands all of those points, will I have achieved the goal I set for this meeting?" Be clear about the mood and emotion you want to convey in your presentation through your tone. For example, hopefulness, enthusiasm, seriousness, celebration, or humor can help project certain moods to your audience.

4. Design a brief opening that takes up about 5% of your total presentation time and allows you to:
   – Present your goals and expectations for the presentation.
   – Clarify the benefits of the presentation to the audience.
   – Explain the overall layout of your presentation.

5. Develop the content and organize your presentation, which should make up about 70-80% of your presentation time.

6. Prepare a brief closing of about 5-10% of your presentation time, which summarizes your presentation's key points.

7. Designate time for questions and answers. This should be the remaining 10% of your presentation time.

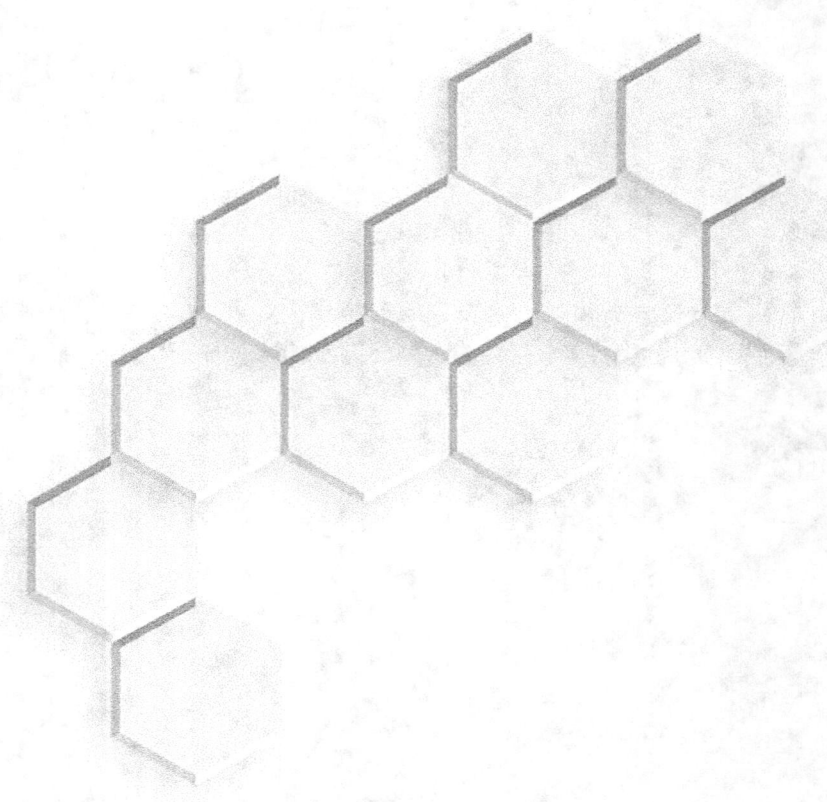

Why Use the Flip Chart?

The flip chart is not "old school." In fact, it is an essential facilitation tool used for annotating during presentations and recording relevant information as it is generated. The most important advantage flip charts have over whiteboards is their ability to facilitate group memory by keeping the pages (adhesive pages) in front of the participants during the session for retention and reference. The concept of group memory involves two elements:

- **Retention and Reference**

    When participants can see the key points of a presentation and have visual access to these flip charts throughout the meeting or discussion, the repeated exposure ensures more excellent retention of the information. Taping flip charts to the walls allows participants to refer to key points while reinforcing them with their own examples and building upon them with new ideas. Participants become more engaged and there is greater group synergy and interaction.

- **Visual Record of Outcomes**

    When the Facilitator records ideas and suggestions on a flip chart as they are mentioned, participants have a visual "memory" of key points as the session progresses. Communication is more precise because of the visual record the flip charts provide. At the meeting's conclusion, participants have a collective memory of agreements and outcomes, whether these are decisions, next steps, or new ideas.

Whiteboards, overhead projectors, and even electronic smart boards with printer capability cannot match the flip chart for generating group memory. You can leave flip charts hanging on the walls for days, allowing participants time to take pictures after a session or to return early the next day to review them. On the other hand, whiteboards are erased as the session continues, and PowerPoint slides are flashed onto the wall and quickly disappear into the darkness.

Facilitation Using Virtual Meeting Rooms™
Distant Training Through Video Conference Technology

As a result of the COVID-19 pandemic, most corporate meetings are now conducted via video conferencing services such as Zoom, Webex, MS Workgroups, Google Workspace, Skype, etc. When it comes to training, video conferencing has become an important communication tool. However, regarding training applications, it is the way we stage the meetings using this technology that will determine the experience outcome and takeaways from the learning sessions.

The Foresight Management Development Program© is a pioneer in the use of video conferencing tools since 2008. We created Virtual Meeting Rooms™ for distant business training when very few organizations knew or used these applications, much less owned the equipment necessary to conduct meetings through professional video conferencing. This technology has come a long way since we developed its application for distance learning, several years ago, mainly due to:

1. the creation of Cloud Computing, which exponentially improved HD video and audio quality,

2. radical improvements in the user friendliness,

3. much quicker logins

4. diminished deployment cost with much less expensive equipment in the market.

Guidelines for Mastering the Use of Video Conferencing for Distance Learning

Unfortunately, the spread of COVID-19 is what made video conferencing widely popular. The need for remote connectivity for communication during corporate business meetings and training sessions became essential to limit contact and infection. Here are some recommendations to help you navigate the use of video conferencing for distance learning:

- If you are the remote Facilitator (host), you will want to have a professional set-up. Invest, at a minimum, in a quality HD camera (with zooming and "follow me" capabilities), a professional microphone, and inexpensive video lighting equipment to improve the quality of the presentation. The use of a laptop webcam is acceptable if you are the participant.

- If you are not hosting the training in a corporate setting, use a simple backdrop, so you do not divert your learners' attention with busy backgrounds. Keep children, pets, and any distractions out of your virtual training room. Virtual background apps such as ChromaCam, help you install all kinds of professional-looking backgrounds for your presentation, however, if you are using flip charts you need to use a pop-up background (examples: https://anyvoo.com).

- Prepare the training material and have it ready at least two weeks in advance, just as you would do with an in-person training session. Ensure each participant receives and prints the training material at least five days before the session, so they can have time to study the content and cases.

- Test the camera and equipment at least 90-minutes before the session. Ensure all the necessary tools, such as microphones, cameras, bandwidth, and software, are operating correctly. If not, you will have plenty of time for troubleshooting. Delaying a video conference due to a technical issue, although sometimes inevitable, is an inconvenience to those waiting to participate and could make the Facilitator look unprofessional and unprepared.

- Run the video conference like an in-person training session. Keep the training session interactive. Use screen-sharing capabilities to engage audience members with plenty of visuals. Also, provide handouts and other materials before the training is scheduled and have them study the material beforehand and use class time to discuss the material.

- Use tent name table cards with the name of participants in bold letters to identify the participants and be able to call them by their name.

- My experience is that the maximum size of your remote video class should not be more than twelve. With a smaller group, you will be able to read facial expressions (with a good professional camera), include the entirety of the group in "round table" discussions, and it is easier to share the microphone, if everyone is in the same location. If people are in remote areas (faces become square tiles in the virtual meeting room), make sure everyone is engaged and participating. It is easy for participants to get sidetracked and search the web while attending the session. So, it would be best if you kept them "on their feet" at all times by asking questions and directing comments toward distracted participants to reengage them in the discussion.

- The Facilitator must speak clearly and ask the participants to do so and use the microphones in the Interactive Virtual Meeting Rooms™. There is a natural tendency for both participants and facilitators to look at the screen, but make sure everyone looks at the camera when speaking. Even though participants are miles away, the technology and interaction bring them into the same virtual classroom where they can learn and communicate as if they are all in the same room.

- Explain the rules and expectations of the classroom, with extra emphasis on noise and distractions. The professional video conferencing microphones are overly sensitive and can pick up small noises and broadcast them to everyone in the session. Even though a Facilitator is not present at all the sites, participants are still expected to behave as if the Facilitator is physically in front of them.

- Once the class session has ended, make sure all equipment is turned off and put away. Find out from the one-site designated personnel what is required to be off before leaving the conference classroom. Cameras and other equipment are expensive, and we need to make sure it is protected and dust-free. Convey to the participants the information required for the next meeting. Post all course materials and handouts online and mail the originals at least ten workdays before each session. Record the session, if possible, for those who missed a class.

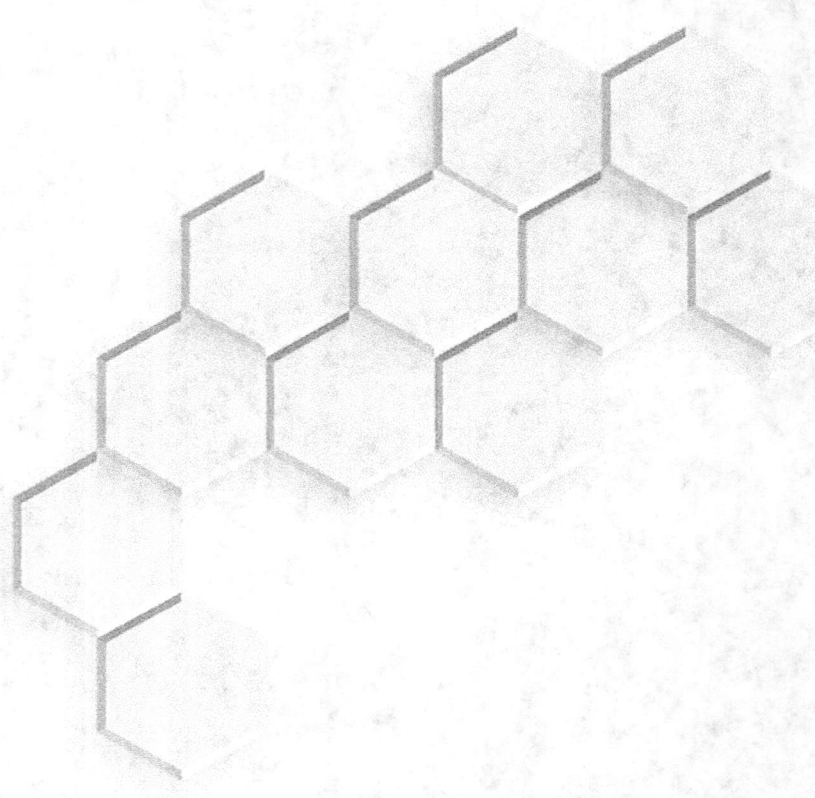

Written Communication

Written communication in the workplace is vital in today's fast-paced environment. Writing is an essential skill because nearly every job requires it to some degree, whether composing emails, memos, or reports. The ability to communicate clearly is necessary so your message can be correctly relayed to your reader.

Tips to Help You Navigate the World of Business Written Communications

- Be clear about your goal and communicate it concisely. You must define the intent of the communication and what you are trying to achieve. For example:
  - What is the purpose of the written communication?
  - What is the specific action you want the person to take?

- Answer the five "W's" of journalism to tell the story: **Who, what, when, where,** and **why**.

- Capture the reader's attention in the first sentence of the first opening paragraph.

- Use familiar words and phrases related to the industry you are communicating about.

- Mention the reader's name and his company throughout the letter.

- Avoid too many "I's" in the letter or, if possible, avoid using this word entirely.

- Use a conversational style.

- Explain what you want the person receiving it to do.
  - Is it to explain or clarify something?
  - Are you just sharing information, or do you want a specific response from them?

- Explain the benefits of responding, as requested.

- Avoid giving the reader a deadline for the response unless required by circumstances or legal purposes. Deadlines may read like an ultimatum. Instead, use something like, "I would appreciate your prompt response."

- Establish credibility and show respect for the reader.

- Be careful with spelling, grammar, and punctuation. Typos are much more tolerated in emails than business letters because people usually understand they are written quickly. However, be aware many people are offended by sloppiness, so always re-read your message before sending it. If time permits, let it sit for 24-hours and edit again before sending it. With this discipline, you may be able to eliminate harmful emotions written on a whim, which could save yourself a lot of grief and embarrassment. Spell-checking your email before sending it is always a wise choice.

- Always show respectful attitudes and language in your communications.

- Have someone else do a quick edit and proofread your letter or report.

- Choose an appropriate communication method. Email is quickly replacing formal business letters in many situations because of the quick turnaround time. Even so, emails are a more informal type of communication and are no substitute for formal communications.

- Email is adequate between people who already have an established relationship. However, when writing to someone you do not know, we suggest taking the time to write a formal business letter for greater effectiveness.

- Never, ever quit your job by email and much worse, by text. This is the coward's media of preference to avoid dealing with sensitive issues face-to-face. In this connected social media world, this unprofessional action may come back to bite you when you are searching for another job.

Use of Letters vs. E-mail vs. Texting

- Use letters for formal communications or if you want to send a communication that will stand out from the multiple emails and texts your receiver gets every day.

- Use e-mail for more informal, quick communications where you need instant answers or attach and send documents. Emails are also good for confirming and scheduling appointments. Never discuss crucial matters over email. Email communications do not convey emotions or facial expressions, therefore, your message can be easily misconstrued, misunderstood, and misinterpreted.

- Use text for making brief statements or when you need instant, timely responses. Never have a conversation using texting, as professionals do not have the time to be texting back and forth, and it becomes an interruption.

References

Armstrong, Patricia. "Blooms Taxonomy." Vanderbilt University Center for Teaching. 2010. https://www.bloomstaxonomy.net/.

Baker, Mary. "9 Future of Work Trends Post-COVID-19." Smarter With Gartner, June 8, 2020. https://www.gartner.com/smarterwithgartner/9-future-of-work-trends-post-covid-19/.

Bloom, Benjamin S., David R. Krathwohl, and Bertram B. Masia. Essay. In *Taxonomy of Educational Objectives: the Classification of Educational Goals: Handbook,* 201–7, 1975.

Calvert, Deb. "Six Preferred Learning Styles for Adults-Adapt Your Message for a Better Response." Managing Americans, 2011. http://www.managingamericans.com/Workplace-Communication-Skills/Success/Six-preferred-learning-styles-for-adults-424.htm.

Candido Segarra; *How to Become a True Professional*

Institute of Canadian Affairs International. "Top Facilitation Competencies." ICA International, June 10, 2019. http://www.ica-international.org/top-facilitation/top-facilitation-competencies/.

Kelly, James. "Learning Pyramid." The Peak Performance Center, September 2012. https://thepeakperformancecenter.com/educational-learning/learning/principles-of-learning/learning-pyramid/.

Kurt, Serhat. "Andragogy Theory - Malcolm Knowles," July 11, 2020. https://educationaltechnology.net/andragogy-theory-malcolm-knowles/.

Marzano, Robert, Debra Pickering, and Jane Pollock. "Classroom Instruction That Works: Research-Based Strategies for Increasing Student Achievement." ERIC. Association for Supervision and Curriculum Development. November 30, 2000. https://eric.ed.gov/?id=ED450096.

UC San Diego. "How to Facilitate Discussions," February 13, 2020. https://blink.ucsd.edu/HR/training/instructor/tools/discussions.html.

Wolowiec, Aaron. "Accounting for 5 Types of Unconscious Bias in Facilitation." Avalon Association Management, March 3, 1970. https://avalonassnmgmt.com/2020/03/16/accounting-for-5-types-of-unconscious-bias-in-facilitation

WSJ Noted. "Here's How the Modern Manager Is Changing." The Wall Street Journal. Dow Jones & Company, January 20, 2021. https://www.wsj.com/articles/heres-how-the-modern-manager-is-changing-11611176412.

Foresight Book Publishing™

ForesightPublishingNow.com

To order copies of these books, please call 423.805.7255
or visit us online at foresightpublishingnow.com

Other Books by
Candido Segarra

www.ingramcontent.com/pod-product-compliance
Lightning Source LLC
Chambersburg PA
CBHW050325120526
44592CB00014B/2047